THE
BEST
AMERICAN
POETRY
1992

◇ ◇ ◇

OTHER VOLUMES IN THIS SERIES

THE
BEST
AMERICAN
POETRY
1992

◇ ◇ ◇

Charles Simic, Editor

David Lehman, Series Editor

COLLIER BOOKS

MACMILLAN PUBLISHING COMPANY

NEW YORK

MAXWELL MACMILLAN CANADA

TORONTO

MAXWELL MACMILLAN INTERNATIONAL

NEW YORK • OXFORD • SINGAPORE • SYDNEY

Collier Books
Macmillan Publishing Company
866 Third Avenue
New York, NY 10022

Maxwell Macmillan Canada, Inc.
1200 Eglinton Avenue East
Suite 200
Don Mills, Ontario M3C 3N1

Macmillan Publishing Company is part
of the Maxwell Communication Group of Companies.

ISBN 0-02-069845-3
ISSN 0-1040-5763

The series editor wishes to express his heartfelt thanks to Kate Fox
Reynolds, his assistant; to Glen Hartley and Lynn Chu, his agents;
and to Erika Goldman, Sharon Dynak, and Charles Flowers of the
Macmillan Publishing Company.

First Collier Books Edition 1992

10 9 8 7 6 5 4 3 2 1

Printed in the United States of America

CONTENTS

David Lehman was born in New York City in 1948. He is the author of two collections of poetry, *An Alternative to Speech* (1986) and *Operation Memory* (1990), both from Princeton University Press. His other books include *Signs of the Times: Deconstruction and the Fall of Paul de Man* (Poseidon Press, 1991) and *The Perfect Murder* (The Free Press, 1989). *The Line Forms Here*, a gathering of his writings on poetry, was recently published by the University of Michigan Press. He has received fellowships from the Guggenheim Foundation and the National Endowment for the Arts, and was selected as a recipient of a 1991 Lila Wallace–Reader's Digest Writer's Award. He lives in Ithaca, New York.

FOREWORD

by David Lehman

◊ ◊ ◊

I remember when the Carter Administration invited several hundred poets to the White House for a celebration of American poetry. There was a reception, handshakes with the president, the pop of flashbulbs. Concurrent poetry readings in various White House rooms capped off the festivities. In each room a few poets had been asked to read. The rest of the poets, the ones who hadn't been asked to read, could attend the reading of their choice. A year later, Jimmy Carter lost the presidency.

I used to think that this incident was a parable for poetry in our time. It seemed to make the point that poets were the only real audience poetry had and that they were implicitly in different camps, having to contend with one another for what little audience there was. I no longer feel so defeatist about poetry's prospects. I believe that American poetry has a true readership beyond its own practitioners and that furthermore it would be impertinent to behave as though this readership were necessarily restricted to an academic ghetto. This is not to deny the existence of a problem but to suggest that perhaps the problem has been ill defined. It is not that American poetry lacks distinction or variety or potential readers; it is that the task of reaching this readership requires a plan as imaginative in its way as the verse on the pages of the books that publishers continue to publish, with reluctance in some cases and with something like ardor in others.

The question of poetry and its audience—with the implicit nagging undertone that maybe poetry doesn't have readers because it doesn't deserve them—has certainly become a hot item in the popular press. Every couple of years an article in a national magazine arouses a good deal of comment by alleging that poetry is dead or by countering this claim with a list of helpful suggestions for improving poetry's public image. In May 1991 Dana Gioia asked readers of the *Atlantic Monthly*, "Can Poetry Matter?" (Gioia recommended that poets recite other poets' works at public readings.) Joseph Brodsky, the nation's new poet laureate, fired off "An Immodest Proposal" in *The New Republic* on Veteran's Day. (Brodsky proposed that an anthology of American poetry be found beside the Bible and the telephone directory in every hotel room across the land.) At Columbia University, three eminent critics pondered "An Audience for Poetry?" with its pointed question mark, while a panel of five poets convened at Adelphi University to discuss "Is Poetry a Dying Art?" On the latter occasion, the moderator ruefully recalled that his title echoed that of Edmund Wilson's famous essay, "Is Verse a Dying Technique?" Wilson published his piece in 1928. Many noble technicians of verse have written since then, and many more will survive the articles and symposia of today, which may even have a salutary effect if they remind people that poetry is, for some of us, a burning issue. Still, all this talk does lead one to wonder whether Oscar Wilde was wrong to suppose that it is easier to do a thing than to talk about it.

The best anthologies are the ones that live up to their names. Each of the five distinguished poets who have served as editors of *The Best American Poetry*—John Ashbery, Donald Hall, Jorie Graham, Mark Strand, and this year Charles Simic—has insisted on excellence as the paramount criterion in the selection process. Each has undertaken the task in an ecumenical spirit. The editors work under few constraints. The poems—never more than seventy-five or fewer than sixty—must come from periodicals published in the previous calendar year. Translations are ineligible, but there are otherwise no deliberate exclusions, and the results can't help reflecting the admirable diversity and abundance of American poetry.

It has been a pleasure working with Charles Simic on *The Best American Poetry 1992*. A marvelous poet writing at the height of his powers, Mr. Simic is also an accomplished essayist, and at the time he and I were collaborating on this project he was working on a monograph about Joseph Cornell—a telling choice, for a Simic poem and a Cornell box illustrate similar principles of juxtaposition and surprise. Both are hospitable to all manner of object and event, and the same may be said about the makeup of this anthology. *The Best American Poetry 1992* includes a "Midwestern Villanelle" and a "Saga" built on sonnet variations, a poem for the New Year and another for All Hallows' Eve, a poem about the jazz trumpeter and singer Chet Baker and one about the fate of eyeglasses in Auschwitz. There is a prose poem by the author of the nation's number-one nonfiction bestseller and a meditation on the color green by a nine-teen-year-old writer living in Vancouver. More than half of the poets in *The Best American Poetry 1992* have not previously appeared in the series. Over three dozen magazines are represented (and numerous others were consulted). Seven titles came from *The New Yorker*, topping the list, and it was a banner year also for *The Paris Review* and *Ploughshares* (six titles each) and for those stalwart campus quarterlies, *The Iowa Review* (five), *Michigan Quarterly Review* and *Field* (four each). The settings range from a women's jail in Rome to the back rooms of a fast-food joint in downtown Milwaukee. And then there are the poems that unabashedly declare their subjects in their titles, such as "Nostalgia" and "Sex," which seem to be our idiomatic equivalents for what T. S. Eliot called "memory and desire."

No critic will ever have the effect on our poets that certain of their grade school teachers had—the ones often credited by the poets themselves for their lifelong devotion to the art. But criticism done right, not vindictively or meanly but with generosity and amplitude, with a respect for the reader's intelligence and the writer's intentions, can help teach us *how* as well as *what* to read, by example rather than by precept. There is no substitute for the sort of poetry criticism that we have so little of at the present time. The contributors' notes in this book—many of which include the poet's comments on his or her poem—are meant not in place of interpretive criticism but as a way of assisting such an effort, and as a bonus for the reader.

From the start, the editors and publishers of *The Best American Poetry* have gone on the assumption that readers equal to the best poetry of the day do exist and will stand up and be counted. It pleases me to report that this seemingly quixotic article of faith has turned out to be a simple statement of fact.

Charles Simic was born in Belgrade, Yugoslavia, in 1938. With his family he emigrated to the United States at the age of sixteen. After attending Ernest Hemingway's alma mater in Oak Park, Illinois, he was drafted into the United States Army and served in West Germany and France before continuing his education at New York University. He has written fourteen books of poems, including *Classic Ballroom Dances* (Braziller, 1980), *Selected Poems: 1963–1983* (Braziller, 1985), and *The Book of Gods and Devils* (Harcourt Brace Jovanovich, 1990). *The World Doesn't End* (Harcourt Brace Jovanovich, 1989), a collection of his prose poems, was awarded the Pulitzer Prize for poetry in 1990. Mr. Simic has published numerous translations of Yugoslav poetry as well as two books in the University of Michigan Press's Poets on Poetry series. He is married, has two children, and teaches at the University of New Hampshire.

INTRODUCTION

by Charles Simic

◇ ◇ ◇

*"I say the word or two that has to be
said . . . and remind every man and woman
of something."*
—WALT WHITMAN

Thirty years ago in New York City I used to stay up late almost every night listening to Jean Shepherd's rambling soliloquies on the radio. He had a show with a lot of interesting talk and a little music. One night he told a lengthy story, that I still remember, about the sacred ritual of some Amazon tribe. It went roughly like this:

Once every seven years, the members of this remote tribe would dig a deep hole in the jungle and lower their finest flute player into it. He would be given no food, only a little water and no way of climbing out. After this was done, the other members of the tribe would bid him good-bye, never to return. Seven days later, the flute player, sitting cross-legged on the bottom of his hole, would begin to play. Of course, the tribesmen could not hear him, only the gods could, and that was the point.

According to Shepherd, who was not above putting on his audience of insomniacs, an anthropologist had hidden himself during the ritual and recorded the man playing the flute. Tonight Shepherd was going to play that very tape.

I was spooked. Here was a man, soon to die, already dizzy with hunger and despair, summoning whatever strength and belief in gods he had. A New World Orpheus, it occurred to me.

Shepherd went on talking until finally, in the wee-hour silence of the night and my shabby room on East Thirteenth Street, the faint sound of the otherworldly flute was heard: its solitary, infinitely sad squeak with the raspy breath of the living human being still audible in it from time to time, making the best of his predicament. I didn't care then nor do I care now whether Shepherd made up the whole story. We are all at the bottom of our own private pits, even here in New York.

All the arts are about the impossible human predicament. That's their fatal attraction. "Words fail me," poets often say. Every poem is an act of desperation or, if you prefer, a throw of dice. God is the ideal audience, especially if you can't sleep or if you're in a hole in the Amazon. If he's absent, so much the worse.

The poet sits before a blank piece of paper with a need to say many things in the small space of the poem. The world is huge, the poet is alone, and the poem is just a bit of language, a few scratchings of a pen surrounded by the silence of the night.

It could be that the poet wishes to tell you about his or her life. A few images of some fleeting moment when one was happy or exceptionally lucid. The secret wish of poetry is to stop time. The poet wants to retrieve a face, a mood, a cloud in the sky, a tree in the wind, and take a kind of mental photograph of that moment in which you as a reader recognize yourself. Poems are other people's snapshots in which we recognize ourselves.

Next, the poet is driven by the desire to tell the truth. "How is truth to be said?" asks Gwendolyn Brooks. Truth matters. Getting it right matters. The realists advise: open your eyes and look. People of imagination warn: close your eyes to see better. There's truth with eyes open and there's truth with eyes closed and they often do not recognize each other on the street.

Next, one wishes to say something about the age in which one lives. Every age has its injustices and immense sufferings, and ours is scarcely an exception. There's the history of human vileness to contend with and there are fresh instances every day to think about. One can think about it all one wants, but making sense of it is another matter. We live in a time in which there are hundreds of ways of explaining the world. Everything, from every variety of religion to every species of scientism, is believed. The task of poetry, perhaps, is to salvage a trace of the authentic from the wreckage of religious, philosophical and political systems.

Next, one wants to write a poem so well crafted that it would do honor to the tradition of Emily Dickinson, Ezra Pound and Wallace Stevens, to name only a few masters.

At the same time, one hopes to rewrite that tradition, subvert it, turn it upside down and make some living space for oneself.

At the same time, one wants to entertain the reader with outrageous metaphors, flights of imagination and heartbreaking pronouncements.

At the same time, one has, for the most part, no idea of what one is doing. Words make love on the page like flies in the summer heat and the poet is merely the bemused spectator. The poem is as much the result of chance as of intention. Probably more so.

At the same time, one hopes to be read and loved in China in a thousand years the same way the ancient Chinese poets are loved and read in our own day, and so forth.

This is a small order from a large menu requiring one of those many-armed Indian divinities to serve as a waiter.

One great defect of poetry, or one of its sublime attractions—depending on your view—is that it wants to include everything. In the cold light of reason, poetry is impossible to write.

Of course, there would be no anthology of best poems if the impossible did not happen occasionally. Authentic poems get written, and that's the best-kept secret in any age. In the history of the world the poet is ever present, invisible and often inaudible. Just when everything else seems to be going to hell in America, poetry is doing fine. The predictions of its demise, about which we read often, are plain wrong, just as most of the intellectual prophecies in our century have been wrong. Poetry proves again and again that any single overall theory of anything doesn't work. Poetry is always the cat concert under the window of the room in which the official version of reality is being written. The academic critics write, for instance, that poetry is the instrument of the ideology of the ruling class and that everything is political. The tormentors of Anna Akhmatova are their patron saints. But what if poets are not crazy? What if they convey the feel of a historical period better than anybody else? Obviously, poetry engages something essential and overlooked in human beings and it is this ineffable quality that has always ensured its longevity. "To glimpse the essential . . . stay flat on your back all day, and moan," says E. M. Cioran. There's more than that to poetry, of course, but that's a beginning.

Lyric poets perpetuate the oldest values on earth. They assert the individual's experience against that of the tribe. Emerson claimed that to be a genius meant "to believe your own thought, to believe that what is true for you in your private heart is true for all men." Lyric poetry since the Greeks has always assumed something like that, but American poetry since Whitman and Emerson has made it its main conviction. Everything in the world, profane or sacred, needs to be reexamined repeatedly in the light of one's own experience.

Here, now, I, amazed to find myself living my life . . . The American poet is a modern citizen of a democracy who lacks any clear, historical, religious or philosophical foundation. Sneering Marxists used to characterize such statements as "typical bourgeois individualism." "They adore the smell of their own shit," a fellow I used to know said about poets. He was a Maoist, and the idea of each human being finding his or her own truth was incomprehensible to him. Still, this is what Robert Frost, Charles Olson, and even Elizabeth Bishop had in mind. They were realists who had not yet decided what reality is. Their poetry defends the sanctity of that pursuit in which reality and identity are forever being rediscovered.

It's not imagination or ideas that our poets primarily trust, but examples, narratives of specific experiences. There's more than a little of the Puritan diarist still left in our poets. Like their ancestors, they worry about the state of their inner lives between entries about the weather. The problem of identity is ever present as is the nagging suspicion that one's existence lacks meaning. The working premise, nevertheless, is that each self, even in its most private concerns, is representative, that the "aesthetic problem," as John Ashbery has said, is a "microcosm of all human problems," that the poem is a place where the "I" of the poet, by a kind of visionary alchemy, becomes a mirror for all of us.

"America is not finished, perhaps never will be," Whitman said. Our poetry is the dramatic knowledge of that state. Its heresy is that it takes a part of the truth for the whole truth and makes it a "temporary stay against confusion," in Robert Frost's famous formulation. In physics it is the infinitely small that contradicts the general law, and the same is true of our poetry at its best. What we love in it is its democracy of values, its variety, its recklessness, its individualism and its freedom. There's nothing more American and more hopeful than our poetry.

"one dark, still Sunday"
—H. D. THOREAU

The black dog on the chain wags his tail as I walk by. The house and the barn of his master are sagging, as if about to collapse with the weight of the sky. On my neighbor's porch and in his yard, there are old cars, stoves, refrigerators, washing machines and dryers that he keeps carting back from the town dump for some unclear and still undecided future use. All of it is broken, rusty, partly dismantled and scattered about, except for the new-looking and incongruous plaster statue of the Virgin with eyes lowered as if embarrassed to be there. Past his house, there's a spectacular winter sunset over the lake, the kind one used to see in paintings sold in back of discount department stores. As for the flute player, I remember reading that in the distant Southwest there are ancient matchstick figures on the walls of desert caves and that some of them are playing the flute. In New Hampshire, where I am now, there's only this dark house, the ghostly statue, the silence of the woods and the cold winter night falling down in a big hurry.

THE
BEST
AMERICAN
POETRY
1992

◇   ◇   ◇

Dance Mania

◇ ◇ ◇

In 1027, not far from Bernburg,
eighteen peasants were seized
by a common delusion.
Holding hands, they circled for hours
in a churchyard, haunted by visions,
spirits whose names they called in terror or welcome,
until an angry priest cast a spell on them
for disrupting his Christmas service,
and they sank into the frozen earth
up to their knees. In 1227
on a road to Darmstadt, scores of children
danced and jumped in a shared delirium.
Some saw devils, others the Savior enthroned
in the open heavens. Those who survived
remained palsied for the rest of their days.
And in 1278, two hundred fanatics raved on a bridge
that spanned the Mosel near Koblenz.
A cleric passed carrying the host
to a devout parishioner, the bridge collapsed,
and the maniacs were swept away.
A hundred years later, in concert with
The Great Mortality, armies of dancers
roved in contortions all over Europe.
The clergy found them immune to exorcism,
gave in to their wishes and issued
decrees banning all but square-toed shoes,
the zealots having declared they hated

pointed ones. They disliked even more
the color red, suggesting
a connection between their malady
and the condition of certain infuriated
animals. Most of all they could not endure
the sight of people weeping.
The Swiss doctor Paracelsus was the first to call
the Church's theories of enchantment
nonsensical gossip. Human life is inseparable
from the life of the universe, he said.
Anybody's mortal clay is an extract
of all beings previously created. Illness
can be traced, he said,
to the failure of the Archaeus, a force
residing in the stomach and whose function
is to harmonize the mystic elements (salt,
sulphur, mercury) on which vitality depends.
He advocated direct measures, proposed remedies
fitting the degree of the affliction.
A patient could make a wax doll of himself,
invest his sins and blasphemies within the manikin,
then burn it with no further ceremony.
He could subject himself to ice-water baths,
or submit to starvation in solitary confinement.
Noted for his arrogance, vanity
and choler (his real name was Theophrastus Bombast
von Hohenheim), Paracelsus made enemies.
They discovered he held no academic degree
and caused him to be banished from Basle,
to become a wanderer who would die mysteriously
at the White Horse Inn in Salzburg in 1541.
After a drunken orgy, said one report.
The victim of thugs hired by jealous apothecaries,
said another. And the dance mania
found its own way through time to survive
among us, as untouched as ever by the wisdom of science.
Think of the strange, magnetic sleep
whole populations fall into every day,

in gymnasiums full of pounding darkness,
in the ballrooms of exclusive hotels,
on verandahs overlooking the ocean and played upon
by moonlight, in backyards, on the perfect lawns
of great estates, on city rooftops, in any brief field
the passing tourist sees as empty—
how many millions of us now, the living
and the dead, hand in hand as always,
approaching the brink of the millennium.

from *The Paris Review*

AGHA SHAHID ALI

I See Chile in My Rearview Mirror

◇   ◇   ◇

By dark the world is once again intact,
Or so the mirrors, wiped clean, try to reason . . .
JAMES MERRILL

This dream of water—what does it harbor?
I see Argentina and Paraguay
under a curfew of glass, their colors
breaking, like oil. The night in Uruguay

is black salt. I'm driving towards Utah,
keeping the entire hemisphere in view—
Colombia vermilion, Brazil blue tar,
some countries wiped clean of color: Peru

is titanium white. And always oceans
that hide in mirrors: when bevelled edges
arrest tides or this world's destinations
forsake ships. There's Sedona, Nogales

far behind. Once I went through a mirror—
from there too the world, so intact, resembled
only itself. When I returned I tore
the skin off the glass. The sea was unsealed

by dark, and I saw ships sink off the coast
of a wounded republic. Now from a blur
of tanks in Santiago, a white horse
gallops, riderless, chased by drunk soldiers

in a jeep; they're firing into the moon.
And as I keep driving in the desert,
someone is running to catch the last bus, men
hanging on to its sides. And he's missed it.

He is running again; crescents of steel
fall from the sky. And here the rocks
are under fog, the cedars a temple,
Sedona carved by the wind into gods—

each shadow their worshipper. The siren
empties Santiago; he watches
—from a hush of windows—blindfolded men
blurred in gleaming vans. The horse vanishes

into a dream. I'm passing skeletal
figures carved in 700 B.C.
Whoever deciphers these canyon walls
remains forsaken, alone with history,

no harbor for his dream. And what else will
this mirror now reason, filled with water?
I see Peru without rain, Brazil
without forests—and here in Utah a dagger

of sunlight: it's splitting—it's the summer
solstice—the quartz center of a spiral.
Did the Anasazi know the darker
answer also—given now in crystal

by the mirrored continent? The solstice,
but of winter? A beam stabs the window,
diamonds him, a funeral in his eyes.
In the lit stadium of Santiago,

this is the shortest day. He's taken there.
Those about to die are looking at him,
his eyes the ledger of the disappeared.
What will the mirror try now? I'm driving,

still north, always followed by that country,
its floors ice, its citizens so lovesick
that the ground—sheer glass—of every city
is torn up. They demand the republic

give back, jewelled, their every reflection.
They dig till dawn but find only corpses.
He has returned to this dream for his bones.
The waters darken. The continent vanishes.

from *Field*

The Ungrateful Citizens

◇ ◇ ◇

It occurs to me that I would like to write a poem about Naples.
Perhaps I have always wanted to do this, and only realized it just
     a moment ago,
but, alas, I have never been to Naples, and yet my desire to write
     about the place
becomes more insuperable by the second. I become convinced that
     my writing desk
is on the same latitude as Naples: I have only to lean back in my chair,
and I incline towards the city of my dreams, and in my dreams my feet
rest in Manhattan while my hair rustles against the wharves of Naples,
and the wharves are bristling with galleons, feluccas, sloops and
     schooners, —
and how blue the sea on which they sway and jostle, how blue the sky
above them, except for some small clumps of cloud so white they
     are like
roses that have seen ghosts! And one could wander forever in the streets
that are as narrow and crooked as the wrinkles on the face of a wise
     and beautiful old woman.
Here all the shop signs are like the titles of arias by Alessandro Scarlatti.
The streets and squares are always busy, yet no one is ever too hurried:
at the slightest opportunity a man or a woman of Naples will sit
     down with you
on some weathered marble doorstep and engage you in the most
     animated conversation
concerning art or politics, your origins, their mother, the latest
     songs or scandals.

A citizen of Naples will say: "Oh, you are from Brooklyn? I have
      a cousin there.
He tells me it is a very beautiful place." He will say this out of pure
      courtesy.
In no other city have I seen so many fragrant pots of flowering
      bergamot,
or such luscious leaves of basil, or so many balconies overhung by
      noble bosoms.
In the late afternoon it is customary for the singers to leave the
      opera house,
and go about their business in full costume: here is the Orfeo of
      Monteverdi
haggling over the price of some pomegranates, and over there
      Donna Elvira
is sipping an espresso in a café while sharing a secret with a
      disheveled Desdemona;
Don Carlos leaves a haberdasher's in a fury while Pinkerton enters
      a tobacconist's,
and Melisande (still in character) weeps beside a baroque public fountain
and here is Poppaea, and Dido, and Ariadne, and Judith, and Violeta . . .
and there goes Madame Butterfly's child eating a fruit like a setting sun
as he saunters down toward the waterfront. There, on the broad
      esplanade,
with its prodigious statuary, many restaurants are to be found,
and they are at once elegant and welcoming. During the heat of the day
their cool marble floors and gently rotating fans are a delight,
and in the evenings entire families go out to dine dressed in the
      finest clothes,
and how charming are the pink and white dresses of the young girls
who resemble gardenias or oleander flowers as they settle lightly
      into their seats.
The families are very large which is why the restaurants are so spacious—
stretching away into shimmering distances in which the fans stir
      the torpid fronds of palms—
and why the menus are as long and varied as the colors of autumn.
Here the generations are nightly conjoined in perfect amity,
and even shy lovers may find corners in which to commune unnoticed
except by some musician who wishes only to urge their love forward

from a tactful distance. The food, it goes without saying, is delicious.
In Naples the taxi drivers have, of necessity, become expert in
      the negotiation
of long flights of stairs resembling formalized cascades,
and the buses constantly circling monuments to heroes of the
      Risorgimento
seem to be dancing a *siciliano* as the sunlight rebounds from their
      windows
and shatters against the high walls of tenements. Beyond those
      walls, however,
in some lightless courtyard a skinny child is crying under lines of
      washing
that repeat, day after day, the same doleful sentence, and I am
      reminded
that this is the city in which songbirds were once blinded so they
      would sing
more poignantly in churches on saints' days, beating against the
      domes and the vaults . . .
and it seems that despite the cheerful beggarwomen and roguish
      merchants
bowed down by enormous, tufted turbans, despite the bravado
of virile gentlemen dressed like eighteenth-century courtesans that I
      had imagined for my Naples,
despite the numberless palaces and paintings, the extravagant
      churches, theaters
and festivals, and the flowers that perfume even the poorest quarters,
it seems that all but the richest and most conservative of citizens
      cannot wait to leave my Naples.
They wish to go to the north or far to the west. They crowd the
      quays and the airport lounges,
and exhibit the horrible condition of their skin, the rags they are
      forced to wear,
the few possessions they drag behind them like so many coffins
      filled with stones.
They glare at me and say: "This is not Naples. This is a place on
      which the world has turned its back.
A cloud of lies covers it. The mansions that you saw are hovels,
      the churches tin shacks,

the parks and gardens, vegetable plots and stony fields in which we
    scratch for a living.
And this is not even the site of wars and massacres, only a place of
    ordinary wretchedness.
No, we cannot be the amorous ballet the tourist requires for a
    backdrop—
O take us away, perhaps to that *island of fragrant grasses* mentioned in
    a fragment of Petronius."

from *The Paris Review*

Poem at the New Year

◇ ◇ ◇

Once, out on the water in the clear, early-nineteenth-century twilight,
you asked time to suspend its flight. If wishes could beget more than
       sobs,
that would be my wish for you, my darling, my angel. But other
principles prevail in this glum haven, don't they? If that's what it is.

Then the wind fell of its own accord.
We went out and saw that it had actually happened.
The season stood motionless, alert. How still the drop was
on the burr I know not. I come all
packaged and serene, yet I keep losing things.

I wonder about Australia. Is it anything like Canada?
Do pigeons flutter? Is there a strangeness there, to complete
the one in me? Or must I relearn my filing system?
Can we trust others to indict us
who see us only in the evening rush hour
and never stop to think? O, I was so bright about you,
my songbird, once. Now, cattails immolated
in the frozen swamp are about all I have time for.
The days are so polarized. Yet time itself is off center.
At least that's how it feels to me.

I know it as well as all the streets in the map of my imagined
industrial city. But it has its own way of slipping past.
There was never any fullness that was going to be;
you stood in line for things, and the soiled light was
impenitent. "Spiky" was one adjective that came to mind,

yet for all its raised or lowered levels I approach this canal.
Its time was right in winter. There was pipe smoke
in cafés, and outside the great ashen bird
streamed from lettered display windows, and waited
a little way off. Another chance. It never became a gesture.

from *The New Yorker*

ROBIN BEHN

Midwestern Villanelle

◊ ◊ ◊

Lately, where my body ends, yours begins.
Or so I keep thinking, although you are far.
It's hard to say, sometimes, just what has been.

To reconstruct the feel of it, give me some men
—all strangers, please—to synchronize the bar
stools' twirling: when the one called *me* winds down you begin

to stir the afternoon. A fifth of gin,
too, please, to symbolize how clear we were
each to each. I know just what has been

between us; it still is. My body here, lupine,
hungry to hear you say how far
it is to where this wanting ends and you begin

the drive back over red, real miles again.
Come back: Galesburg, known for trains, Star-
lite Motel where giant neon lips flash *What's Been*

Can Be Again. There's a compass in
your body. My open legs? Your two-point star
that lights up where our one body ends. Or else begins:
beneficent, hard to hold, just what's always been.

from *The Iowa Review*

How I Painted Certain of My Pictures

◇   ◇   ◇

"You say I'm like a Jewish mother but the kid

is losing weight." Turning by turns as though

turns would make it different. Sunny

with shallows all about, the solvent

flush of fiduçiary abandon. Mayhem

that may be all right for Craig or

Thomas but makes Dora duller. *By crater*

lakes, the minds too late. Or do the

pushed pins pullulate; not that

the motivation to continue could ever be

just go on. Ingratiatingly grouchy, guardedly

unconscious. Or else the pride of admission

is not worth spitting on. *I got to*

gargle but the loop's on the VCR

& the pillow's in deep

fry. Similar

to dusting for fiberboard after each

feel. "I

don't like mistakes, but purposes

truly scare me." The lorry has left the

levy lest the sandwiches lay

lost, looted.

Which cries out suddenly, incorrigibly

that the gasket's blown an apricot. Or

there'll be no more glowing. As in

a deed is worth only half a word, over

three-foot bird (seldom

blurred). & then

the launches sway in the cringe, fix

flutters against green & yellow

mutters (mothers). "Thomas

is in my place & won't

move." But it's not birds

that are the problem. As if the

ordinary

where just there answering

our call but we

won't sound it

out, or find the work

too demanding (de-

meaning), too extra

ordinary. There

are sleigh bells I know but never

mine. Yet nothing I've lost, nothing

yet to

find. If that makes you sad

then I'm sad too, even though we've

never met or meet just now. Events

are no protection from circumstance

& circumstance is a positive hindrance.

Darling girl, darling boy
Let's burn the house
Tear down the ploys

Stalled among the pantomimes,

obsolete rimes. Never saw a bird

that didn't want to fly—but there must be

pigeons of different feather. Yet woman & man

are no feather at all. Crazy like this

rag gun rapping on my brain's floor.

So skip to the slaughter
Just like you ought'er
& take that smirk off your grimace

Yet kindness has such a bad

name, deliverance no less. Trees won't

say it any better than "O!"

rings. Every syllable stings. & that's the

hardest thing to stomach on a low-noise

diet, if you can sink your teeth into

the

thought that all that sound gotta be

digested. Anemic

poetry—or roughage?—for the health-

continent society? But

why prize distraction over direction, song over

solemnity? The times detail a change of

pockets & everybody's loopy, mind made

up with hospital corners, while the leaves

of our lives unsettle their occupation. Or

is it a value simply to glide in the

turbulent air & push back when things

get foreshortened? The fate of the earth—

like if the world doesn't care who will?

"Don't scream so close my face!"

That we have to inhabit the world to know where

the earth might be, *is*. Then where was

it (was it?) lost. When I get

home I'll glue it together as a little book.

& if that won't work we can play Billie-

come-gravely all the way to the moon. *If*

the clue slips tear it. Nor jingle your

jaundiced gestures in my directions.

I'm as plump as a cherry on the tree

George Washington never chopped, as carefree

as a hornet in amphetamine

dive. You'll

be lucky if you get out of here with your

yarmulke intact—but the shadow world will

intervene before the last lost moment. "People

don't like you because you're a brat—selfish

& whiny." Although if you brush your teeth

twice you'll get more than enough advice.

"I had to leave the job because I couldn't

stand the people & the work was totally

absorbing." Because humble is not

the same as

humiliated.

Notice which bugs.

& over & over again

with aesthetic turpitude

(Let's trade flavors).

Normally I'd say there was no jettisoning.

But my friend Frisby-Love took all she could take

before dead-ending the herbervescent poker

patch. Darn this dated elan, these holes

of pure cheesecloth. *As if outside*

were anywheres at all. Bruised to the knees

in amours & cleaves. Confidence

just a prick—the man

on the barge selling

you the bridge between this thought

&

this.

Still waters run about as deep

as you can blow them. But it's time

I came clean & you swept the boat

(I mean cameo): floor-length conscription

with matching five-piece hush-orange ensemble.

Reading the riot act in the middle of

sacral pacts. "Whatever you say,

Sheriff!" "It's been a long day,

they always are." "But why can't I

go out because I can see children

playing?" Fluent in dreams, inconsolable

otherwise. "I guess I have you

to thank

for the mustard." I guess

we all just

want to go home to bed.

I guess

light doesn't even notice

it's going so fast.

Drum beats on the meridian, sun beats on the

Mercedes. Mr. Bush stares blankly

on the podium wondering what to do next. M.

Mitterand has some warm words for Danton. Mrs.

Thatcher bangs a few notes on her bagpipe.

The silencers click onto

the muzzles.

"I just don't want

to have to

go through that again."

I'll

just put down my

pen.

Exeunt.

Curtain.

ACTION!

from *Hambone*

Healing

◇ ◇ ◇

The girl I love still sleeps with her mother
who is huge, bulky as a bear.
It is a small house in Guthrie
without a doorknob or a father.
He is silent on a hill. They forget
to leave flowers on Memorial Day.

We stay up late, kissing in the car,
windows open to the cricket buzz.
Inside, her mother barely sleeps.
Food goes bad in the fridge.
The worthless brother, guitar
plugged to the wall, wails.

The boom's gone bust.
Every other house
is empty in this neighborhood,
a democracy of failure.
Armadillos rustle in the brush.
We watch the neighbors tune their truck,
the breasts of a woman they saw
in a bar last night troubling
the pure mechanics of their talk.

All day the brother sleeps
in his leaking waterbed.
The father, a stern man
in uniform, watches me
from the bookshelf.

Her hair is perfectly black
and smells faintly of her permanent.
I walk to the drugstore with her
to buy artificial nails. They leave
red highways down my spine.
In the sink her dishes grow
green. The back yard rises
in a weedy funk, foaming
over bones of old cars.
The dog drowns in ticks.

An aunt comes by, ashen-faced.
This is a laying on of hands.
Her tumor's growing like a great idea,
a central concept. Jesus,
everyone says, their palms
burning through to the core. Heal.
A cousin wears Christ
on a t-shirt: this blood's for you.
Pepsi's in the fridge.

Soaps in the afternoon, couples
humping through the broadcast day.
In the glamor magazines
scattered on the floor
women tan and tone.
They come hard with famous men.
I suggest we go

for a doorknob at the hardware store.
Vetoed. Too hot.
A sister visits, baby

sucking at her chest.
She swears her milk
will shoot across the room.

At dusk we drive to the Sonic,
a neon bonfire near
the base's barbed perimeter.
B-52s tilt over with a black wake.
Evil, she says, munching okra,
her face so beautiful
in the red fire of sunset
my throat tightens, I could cry.
A song comes over the radio,
the very car shimmers, the bulbs
of the drive-in blooming
red and blue, deepening
in the failing light
and she moves into my arms,
smelling of soap and french fries.
All around us
men and women, boys and girls
are tuned to the same frequency,
moving together under the tinted glass,
beneath the whirlwind of moths
in the hot air, the Sonic
throbbing with light and love,
the life I left to come here
forgotten and the sun
sliding down a dome of gold.
She laughs. Mosquitoes
rise in the rural haze.
Her tongue is in my ear.

from *The Iowa Review*

"Dear, My Compass . . ."

◇ ◇ ◇

Dear, my compass
still points north
to wooden houses
and blue eyes,

fairy-tales where
flaxen-headed
younger sons
bring home the goose,

love in hay-lofts,
Protestants, and
heavy drinkers . . .
Springs are backward,

but crab-apples
ripen to rubies,
cranberries
to drops of blood,

and swans can paddle
icy water,
so hot the blood
in those webbed feet.

—Cold as it is, we'd
go to bed, dear,
early, but never
to keep warm.

from *The New Yorker*

ROBERT BLY

The Crippled Godwit

◇   ◇   ◇

Shorebirds occupy a patch of sand near the ocean. Eighteen or twenty godwits work, driving their long frail beaks into sand recently made slate-colored by the falling tide. A dozen turn their backs to the surf and walk inland, striding on legs purposeful and thin. Their abrupt walk integrates motions that seem contrary to us, as when a jerking branch somehow joins the flow of the river. Now the flock feeds again—each lifts the head briefly to swallow, then drives the bill back into sand; when the bill is down, the whole body shakes, the tail feathers bob up and down. Each time the head lifts, the eyes are black, calm, alert, keeping watch . . .

One godwit, not as plump as the others, stands balanced on one leg, the other drawn up. My breath pauses as I notice that the foot is missing, and in fact the whole leg below the knee is gone. When he hops, his isolated knee bends like the other one; his single foot kicks a little sand away with each step. Feeding and hopping, he comes up near one of the plump ones, and with a swift motion, perfectly in rhythm, bites him in the ass. He then hops out of the flock and feeds alone.

It took me so long to notice that one bird was not a real member of the flock, which moves continually, striding or flying. Sometimes the group strides away and leaves him; at other times feeds around him. The flock rises once more and flies toward the sea where the packed sand shines. The bird with one leg rises with them, but turns in the air, his long wings tipping among the winds, and lands at his old place to feed alone.

from *Ploughshares*

Inevitably, She Declined

◇　◇　◇

On a bishop's backless chair, inevitably, upright she declined
Watching an empire flicker & die out. Morning, an anodyne
Of undrugged sleep, her attendant files the wedding ring embedded
In her flesh for half a century, an unhinged sapphire unmarrying
A monarch to this life of beautiful bastard sovereignty, unwedding
England's bloated hand. By evening an heirless country waits to bury
A distended queen with hawthorn boughs, bonfires blazing majusculed
Letters in the streets. She will go on watching them, upright &
    inevitable.
When Elizabeth sat dying, she would not lie down, for fear
She would never rise again, her high neck propped with molecules
Of lace, circling a countenance decked with the small queer
Embellishments of monarchy. In a breathless hour, her virguled
Breath, a speechless pilgrim grateful for a little death, minuscule
Between moments, squall of air reclining, upright bolt, declining
    vertical.

from *Michigan Quarterly Review*

Homage to Gerolamo Marcello

◊   ◊   ◊

Once in winter I, too, sailed in
here from Egypt, believing that I'd be greeted
on the crowded quay by my wife in resplendent furs
and a tiny veiled hat. Yet I was greeted
not by her but by two small, decrepit
Pekinese with gold teeth. Their German owner
told me later that, should he be
robbed, the Pekinese might help him
to make ends meet; well, at least initially.
I was nodding and laughing.

The quay was infinite and completely
vacant. The otherworldly
winter light was turning palazzi into porcelain crockery
and the populace into those who won't
dare to touch it.
Neither veil nor, for that matter, furs
were at issue. The sole transparent
thing was the air and its pinkish, laced
curtain in the hotel "Meleagres and Atalanta,"
where, as far back as then, eleven years ago,
I could have surmised, I gather,
that the future already
had arrived. When a man's alone,
he's in the future—since it can manage
without the supersonic stuff,

streamlined bodies, an executed tyrant,
crumbling statues; when a man's unhappy,
that's the future.
                    Nowadays I don't get
on all fours any longer in the hotel
room, imitating its furniture and safeguarding
myself against my own maxims. Now to die of grief
would mean, I'm afraid, to die
belatedly, while latecomers
are unwelcome, particularly in the future.

The quay swarms with youngsters chattering in Arabic.
The veil has sprouted into a web of rumors,
dimmed later into a net of wrinkles.
And the Pekinese long ago got consumed by their canine Auschwitz.
No sign of the owner, either. What seems to have survived
is but water and me, since water also
has no past.

                    from *The New Yorker*

_____
31

Sex

◇ ◇ ◇

On the first few nights of the new year, a week
   ago, we had a full moon or near it in central
New York and the air was cold, the snow frozen,
   metallic, and bright. On the steep field
the stream of moonlight flowed down from the crest
   of the hill to the little house. A frozen stream,
he thought—the man I am always writing about.
   But when he looked more closely he saw, or
thought he saw, the molecules of light flowing
   both ways in scarcely discernible swiftness,
down to him, up to the moon, reflected glints
   in a flux of passionate intensity in a pure
world, a simple world, his peaceful valley. He was
   thinking about sex. He was thinking especially
of last night when he had been in bed with the
   young woman he called conventionally, as people
do, *his*, and he had been saddened. Aging men
   suffer two kinds of impotence, the ordinary
kind that everyone makes jokes about, and then
   the deeper psychic failure when they are full
of eros, but it is hidden, too remote
   to evoke the wonder of lust in their partners.
So it had been, and then afterward they lay
   looking out at the moontrack on the snow.
Now he is alone in his house with his gray
   neutered cat Pokey. In former times women

who would not heat up were made into slaves,
    and when too many slaves encumbered the
polity, these women were lowered into
    wells until they drowned. Nor was this some
stewpot of Asian hillbillies in the *National
    Geographic*, but in Europe, a nation I do not care
to name. Pokey, on the table next to the Christmas
    cactus, was looking out the glass door, staring
at the moontrack with his yellow eyes immense,
    unmoving, until the spell was broken and he
glided down like a shadow and went to the kitchen
    where he fizzed the litter in his box. Is it
that aging people live in an assortment
    of remnants, impulses too worn, desires
too flaccid to function any more? The man
    felt all his love gathering outside him, a power
with no bodily counterpart, out there in the
    deathly cold, in the ghostly light, as if
the beautiful young woman in her nakedness
    were a circumstance of the night, seen
in the time of unseeing. For many moments
    he looked out at the moon and the moonflow,
at the dark woods on either side, at the frozen
    snow, until finally he too went into the shabby
kitchen and opened the door of an upper cabinet,
    and took down a jar of peanut butter. Death
may come in many forms, they say, but truly
    it comes in only one, which is the end of love.
The clock on the big oaken bookcase, still running
    after sixty-nine years, strikes one in the morning,
a clanking tone, ice falls from the eaves—changes
    in the night. The cat rubs against the man's legs.

from *The Sewanee Review*

Nostalgia

◊ ◊ ◊

Remember the 1340's? We were doing a dance called the Catapult.
You always wore brown, the color craze of the decade,
and I was draped in a cape with pomegranates in needlework.
Everyone would pause for beer and onions in the afternoon.
And at night we would play a game called "Find the Cow."
Announcements were hand-lettered then, not like today.

Where has the summer of 1572 gone? Brocade and sonnet
marathons were the rage. We used to dress up in the flags
of rival baronies and conquer one another in cold stone rooms.
Out on the dance floor we were doing the Struggle.
Alone in her room your sister would practice the Daphne for hours.
We borrowed the jargon of farriers for our slang.
These days words seem transparent, a code everyone has broken.

The 1790's will never come again. Childhood was big.
People would take walks to the very tops of hills
and write everything down in their journals without speaking.
Our collars were very high and our hats were very soft.
We would surprise each other with alphabets made of twigs.
It was a great time to be alive, or even dead.

I am also fond of the period between 1815 and 1821.
Europe was trembling but we were having our portraits done.
1901 is a year I would love to return to, if only briefly,
time enough to wind up a music box and do a few dance steps.

Or take me back to 1922, 1941, or 1957, or at least
let me recapture the mood of last month when we picked
berries and glided through afternoons in a canoe.

Even this morning would be an improvement on the present.
I was in the garden, then, surrounded by the hum of bees
and the Latin names of flowers, watching the early light
flash off the slanted windows of the greenhouse
and gild the needles on the limbs of dark hemlocks.

As usual, I was thinking about the past
whose moments were stones on the bottom of a stream
and my memory was the water rushing over them.
I was even thinking a little about the future, that place
where people are doing a dance we cannot imagine,
a dance whose name we can only guess.

from *The Georgia Review*

Other

◇ ◇ ◇

Having begun in thought there
in that factual embodied wonder
what was lost in the emptied lovers
patience and mind I first felt there
wondered again and again what for
myself so meager and finally singular
despite all issued therefrom whether
sister or mother or brother and father
come to love's emptied place too late
to feel it again see again first there
all the peculiar wet tenderness the care
of her for whom to be other was first fate.

from *Grand Street*

Famous Women— Claudette Colbert

◊ ◊ ◊

He was quite a guy how he laughed like oh what's the name of the guy
He said dude he said babe he said dude he said babe
Just as a stork flew by
Like he knows which is which?

The treatment: Who's to know which is which?

It was a warm Hollywood night
Tongue hanging warmth
The kinda warmth that makes asphalt turn into grainy black hair
The kind Claudette Colbert wore in oh what's the name of the movie

The studio got him a dummy and oh what a dummy
Someone stuck Claudette Colbert into the trunk of his Olds
Really cruel people, the kind you don't want to meet
Stuck her in his trunk
Really cruel people played a trick on a starry-eyed kid
Initiated for the first time on the LA freeway
The entrances and exits and all the guys behind you laughing
Kinda makes you nervous

How about exploding palm trees!
How about the stork carrying newborn dudes and babes to Universal!
It kinda makes you nervous the first time out
Kinda like how it felt with oh what was the name of that girl

So away he went doing wheelies down the Santa Monica
This was the great love affair of the Western World
He and Claudette chugging on a steamy evening oh so steamy until
The back of the trunk burst into flames like palm trees
Kinda made him nervous

He pulled to the side and fanned the flames
But it was too hot, baby
So he started thumbing for a ride
Like Clark Gable in oh what's the name of that—

It's plastic now.
The back of the Olds, Claudette was plastic after all a plastic dummy
Kinda makes you nervous, huh?
Plasticky melted fleshy bubbly poly peptide urethane all over the
chrome bumper sloppy on the license plate tail lights
A big plastic fleshy mess, the whole back of the Olds looks like
a big fleshy ass

Which is which?

What a sight for such a new boy in town
A faceless new boy new born
The stork carried him
Things like that always happen here
Never got real famous but close enough and at least he was happy
Not that we can tell which was which

from *Fine Madness*

CARL DENNIS

Spring Letter

◇ ◇ ◇

With the warmer days the shops on Elmwood
Stay open later, still busy long after sundown.
It looks like the neighborhood's coming back.
Gone are the boarded storefronts that you interpreted,
When you lived here, as an emblem of your private recession,
Your ship of state becalmed in the doldrums,
Your guiding stars obscured by fog. Now the cut-rate drugstore
Where you stocked your arsenal against migraine
Is an Asian emporium. Aisles of onyx, silk, and brass,
Of reed baskets so carefully woven and so inexpensive
Every house could have one, one work of art,
Though doubtless you'd refuse, brooding instead
On the weavers, their low wages and long hours,
The fruit of their labor stolen by middlemen.
Tomorrow I too may worry like that, but for now
I'm focusing on a mood of calm, a spirit of acceptance,
Loyal to my plan to keep my moods distinct
And do each justice, one by one.
The people in line for ice cream at the Sweet Tooth
Could be my aunts and uncles, nieces and nephews.
What ritual is more ancient or more peaceable?
Here are the old ones rewarding themselves
For making it to old age. Here are the children
Stunned into silence by the ten-foot list of flavors
From Mud Pie to Milky Way, a cosmic plenty.
And those neither young nor old, should they be loyal
To their favorite flavor or risk a new one?

It's a balmy night in western New York, in May,
Under the lights of Elmwood, which are too bright
For the stars to be visible as they pour down on my head
Their endless starry virtues. Nothing confines me.
Why you felt our town closing in, why here
You could never become whoever you wished to be,
Isn't easy to understand, but I'm trying.
Tomorrow I may ask myself again if my staying
Is a sign of greater enlightenment or smaller ambition.
But this evening, pausing by the window of Elmwood Liquors,
I want to applaud the prize-winning upstate Vouvray,
The equal of its kind in Europe, the sign says.
No time for a glass on your search
As you steer under stars too far to be friendly
Toward the island where True Beauty, the Princess,
Languishes as a prisoner. I can see you at the tiller
Squinting through the spume, hoping your charts are accurate,
Hoping she can guess you're on your way.

from *Poetry*

My Amaryllis

◇ ◇ ◇

So this is the day the fat boy learns to take the jokes
by donning funny hats, my Amaryllis,
my buffoon of a flower,
your four white bullhorn blossoms like the sirens
in a stadium through which the dictator announces he's in love.
Then he sends out across the land a proclamation—
there must be music, there must be stays of execution
for the already dying.
That's how your pulpy sex undoes me and your seven
leaves, unsheathed. How you diminish
my winter windows, and beyond them, the Atlantic.
How you turn my greed ridiculous.
Now it's as if I could believe in having children after forty,
or, walking these icy streets, greet sullen strangers
like a host of former selves, so ask them in, of course,
and listen like one forgiven to their crimes.
Dance with us and all our secrets,
dance with us until our lies,
like death squads sent to an empty house, put down,
finally, their weapons, peruse the family
portraits, admire genuinely the bride.
Stay with me in this my exile
or my returning, as if to love the tyrant one more time.

O my lily, my executioner, a little stooped, here,
listing, you are the future bending
to kiss the present like a sleeping child.

from *Ploughshares*

Smiles

◇ ◇ ◇

It was as if a pterodactyl had landed,
   cocky
and fabulous amid the earth-bound,

so it's not difficult to understand
   why I smiled
when I saw that Rolls Royce

moving slowly on the Black Horse Pike
   past the spot
where Crazy Eddie's once was.

Just one week earlier I'd seen a man,
   buttoned-downed and wing-tipped,
reading *Sonnets to Orpheus* in paperback

at the mall's Orange Julius stand.
   My smile was inward,
I craved some small intimacy,

not with him, but with an equal lover
   of the discordant,
another purchaser adrift among the goods.

Sometimes I'd rather be ankle-deep
   in mud puddles,
swatting flies with the Holsteins,

I'd rather be related to that punky boy
   with purple hair
walking toward the antique shop

than to talk with someone who doesn't know
   he lives
in *"Le Siècle de Kafka,"* as the French

dubbed it in 1984. The State of New Jersey
   that same year,
refused to pay Ai for a poetry reading

 because her name needed two more letters,
   which produced my crazy smile,
though I wanted to howl too, I wanted to meet

the man who made the rule, kiss him hard
   on his bureaucratic lips,
perhaps cook for him a scalding bowl

of alphabet soup. Instead we added two asterisks
   and the check came!
Four spaces on a form all filled in

and the State was pleased, which is why
   I'm lonely
for the messiness of the erotic, lonely

for that seminal darkness that lurks
   at birthday parties, is hidden
among hugs at weddings, out of which

smiles, even if wry or bitter, are born.
   In the newspaper today
it says that the man who robbed a jewelry store

in Pleasantville, crippling the owner,
    wan't happy
with his life, was just trying to be happier.

And in Cardiff, just down the road, someone
    will die at the traffic circle
because history says so, history says *soon*,

and that's the circle I must take
    in my crushable Toyota
if I wish to stay on the Black Horse Pike,

and I do.

from *The Iowa Review*

The Bright Waterfall of Angels

◇　◇　◇

Everywhere that summer there were angels,
hanging over the lake piers deflated with prayer,
blowing like soap bubbles past night windows,
flying from the weekend colored skirts
of young girls. In August, under the full
moon, I walked Oakland Ave., and a night
bus, windows burning yellow with angels, passed.
And still, I could see people praying for more
bird angels, drug angels, kaiser roll angels, money
angels, love angels, health angels, rain angels.
There were angels with hearts large as bagpipes
who circled our village's ice cube houses
and flew bright loud into our bang nights.
There were angels in movie houses and in sweet corn
stands, and angels who dropped like catalpa
snakes from summer. One angel followed
me into our Chang Cheng Restaurant. Where
were the angels that summer when the neighbor-
hood women were being hunted and ripped
open like field animals? Or when the man
who walked away from DePaul Rehab gave up
on my garage? When I came home from "The Wizard
of Loneliness" the Flight for Life
helicopter was landing in my front yard.
And a young man was leaning against my garage,
his throat an awful open clown smile.
Rivers and streams of dark blood

ran down the alley. All the children
awakened by the helicopter ran barefoot
and pajamad through the actual
blood and night. Mary,
the neighborhood nurse, kept telling
everyone there was a murderer loose.
"No one could do that much damage to themselves.
I'm a nurse, I'm telling you that no one could
do that much damage to themself."
And the police, and firefighters, and pilot,
and attendants their rubber gloved hands filled
with the moon, and someone held up the knife
the man had used on himself. Off they rolled
him on a cot into the helicopter.
When they took off lighted and loud into the mid-
night sky, I saw angels of despair, windfull
and spinning happy on the helicopter blades.
There were angels who wrote their names on leaves,
and show-offs who rode August's tornadoes.
Nights the sky was often a thunder of angels,
a heat lightning sky, where angel wings fit
together in crossword puzzle perfection.
At the State Fair that August, the great
chefs of Wisconsin came to convince the world
of the superior beauty of carved cheese over carved
ice for table centerpieces, and although originally
they had come planning to carve cows and swans,
always the cheddar blocks turned to the gold
cheesy beauty of angels. Angels hid
behind apples, behind goldfinches, hid in foot-high
Mexican-stuffed toads who stood forever on
their back legs, their front legs shellacked forever
into playing red painted concertinas.
And if someone would have come to you as many
years as you are old ago, and told you:
You will be slapped around, a man will cut your
mouth open, only because he says he loves you,
and you will have to give up lovers, before they are,

and children before they are yours;
friends will call you from sexual assault centers
and their stitched together voices will tell you
things done to them that you will never be able to forget.
Some friends you will bury and children and parents, too.
(Your mother and father will breathe flowers
from their graves.) Your body's skin and bones
will cartwheel around you, tilt-a-whirl around you
until you are nauseous and dizzy and uncertain.
The money angel will never like you; often
you will sleep with razor blades. Often
you will fall out of the trap door of yourself
and have to climb back up and start over, and
sometimes the angels will help and often they won't,
and you can never count on either. And if someone
had come to you, as many years ago as you are old
right now, and told you all this, and more,
would you sign up for the bright waterfall of angels?
Would you be silent? Would you whisper, or shout:
Bring on the tour, the bright waterfall of angels tour?

from *The Iowa Review*

A Little Heart-to-Heart
with the Horizon

◇　◇　◇

Go figure—it's a knitting performance every day,
keeping body and clouds together,
the sky grounded. Simulcast, ecumenical
as everywhere, stay and hedge
against the bet of bouffant space,
you're the binding
commitments so worlds won't split.

Last week we had Thanksgiving.
The post-cold warriors held a summit
full of East meets West
high hopes. Why not hold a horizon?
Something on the level, equitable instead.
They said the U.S. Army held rehearsals
on monastic sand. In the desert,
lieutenants zipped in camouflage
thought back to where horizons were
an unmade bed, a nap
on the world's edge. Privates, nights
when they were sanded
by flower fitted sheets, ground out
in flower fitted skin: her, oh him.

This Michigan is short on mountains,
long on derricks
needlenosing heaven, making evil
electromagnetic fields.
"Talks on the fringes of
the summit could eclipse
the summit itself," the anchor
admitted. Go figure.

Your reticence, your serene
lowness, because of you I have something
in common with something.
Your beauty is *do unto me* and who am I
to put you in the active voice?
I rest my case
in your repose, a balance
beam, point
blank closure
that won't—bows are too ceremonious—

close. You graduate
in lilac noise. You take off
and you last.
You draw all conclusions
and—erasure, auroral—you
come back. But I am here to vanish
after messing up the emptiness.
I am here to stand
for thanks: how it is
given, hope: how it is
raised. I am here to figure
long division—love—
how it is made.

from *Ploughshares*

TESS GALLAGHER

We're All Pharaohs
When We Die

◇　◇　◇

Our friends die with us
　　and the sky too
　　　　　in huge swatches, and lakes, and places
　　　　　　we walked past, just going and
　　　　　　　　coming.
The spoons we ate with look dim, a little deadened
　　in the drawer. Their trips to the mouth
　　　　　forlorn, and the breath caught there
　　　　　　　fogged to a pewtery smudge.

Our friends die with us and are thrown in because we
used them so well.
But they also stay on earth awhile like the abandoned
　　huts of the Sherpas on a mountain that doesn't know
　　　　　it's being climbed. They don't fall down all at once.
　　　　　　　　Not like his heart
fell down, dragging
the whole gliding eternity of him out of sight.

Guttural and aslant, I chew the leather sleeve
　　of this jacket, teething like a child on the unknown pressure
　　　　　budding near its tongue. But the tongue
　　　　　　　　is thrown in too, everyone's who said his name
as he used to be called
in our waking and sleeping,

dreaming and telling the dreams.
Yes, the dreams are thrown in
so the mystery
breaks through still wearing its lid, and I am never
to be seen again
out of his muslin striding.

If this is my lid then, with its eyebrows painted on, with its
stylized eyes glazed open above the yet-to-be-dead ones, even so
a dead-aliveness looks through
as trees are thrown in
and clouds and the meadows under the orchards
the deer like to enter—those returning souls
who agree to be seen
gazing out of their forest-eyes
with our faint world painted over them.

from *The Paris Review*

On Wanting to Grow Horns

◊   ◊   ◊

Man's envy of animals is ancient,
a damp cave filled to the rafters
with handsome pallid bats, lemurs,
beetles, mallards. *Do I really
have to walk upright all the time?*
Swooping lucidly, melancholy enters
the mind through one's nasal
passages, like the homey smell
of burnt pot roast. Male fruit bats
court females by honking, and flashing
tufts of fur on their shoulders:
not such strange behavior. Less
comprehensibly, child murder's
on the rise. A fly grazes the dog's hide,
which shivers. Primitive brain surgery
involved poking a hole in the sufferer's
skull, a cranial skylight through which
blinding pain or hallucinations
could escape. Sometimes it worked.
Flatworms just grow new heads when needed.
I wear my learned helplessness pinned
to my blouse like a spider's egg sac,
in lieu of your corsage. Brush against me
and it'll rupture, spilling pale
pollen-like spiders. Elephants
ransacked the hunters' tent,
removed a pile of ivory tusks

and buried them. Fascinating to be yanked
out of bed by strange hands.
Vultures can fly 90 miles per hour.
He pulled the quilt tighter
around him, mistaking its stripes
for protective coloring. Male
butterflies and moths can smell
females miles away. *For Christ's sake,*
it was just a love-bite. Sponges
may follow the shapes of rocks
over which they grow. You can't
receive medical attention
at this facility. If a rabbit warren
becomes too crowded, pregnant rabbits
absorb their fetuses till there's
more room. He wakes each morning
feeling like a sore that won't heal.
Pelicans unite to drive fish
into shallow water where they're
more easily caught. For our soundtrack,
we thought of using a tape of inmates
gibbering as they defaced gravestones,
dug up and scattered the bones of those
they hated. Imagine that tenacity:
to despise your enemies' skeletons,
savoring rancor toward brittle rods
of calcium. Ranks and classes
are highly developed among insects.
Each time I pay my rent, my hoarse
landlord growls: "My dentist's jewish.
My lawyer's jewish. There are so many
of you." The dog lies quietly
by the stove, gnawing a cow's hoof
I have given her. My mother claims
I was born with a tail, cut off
by some short-sighted obstetrician.

from *Witness*

JACK GILBERT

Voices Inside and Out

◇   ◇   ◇

for Hayden Carruth

When I was a child, there was an old man with
a ruined horse who drove his wagon through the back
streets of our neighborhood crying, *Iron . . . iron.*
Meaning he would buy bedsprings and dead stoves.
Now it seems a blazon for the primitive Pittsburgh
of rusted metal and dirty air, and people drinking
Iron City beer. Meaning for me in the years since
the mind's steel and the riveted girders of the soul.
And whatever it is sometimes in love for which I have
given big chunks of my life. When I was a young man
living in the Nineteenth Century of the Ile Saint-Louis,
a glazier came every morning along the street that ran
through the center of the island crying, *Vitrine . . .*
vitrine, meaning the glass on his back, but sounding
like the swallows swooping at evening in the high air
years later outside my room in Perugia. In my boyhood
summers, Italian men came walking ahead of the truck
calling out the ripeness of their melons, and ancient
Jewish men slogged in the snow crying, *Brooms . . . brooms.*
Two hundred years ago, the London shop boys yelled
at people going by, *What do you lack?* A terrible
question to face every day. "Less and less," I think.

55

The Brazilians say, In this country we have everything we need, except what we don't have. And maybe that is the answer for me now as I begin to walk away.

from *Ploughshares*

LOUISE GLÜCK

Vespers

◊ ◊ ◊

In your extended absence, you permit me
use of earth, anticipating
some return on investment. I must report
failure in my assignment, principally
regarding the tomato plants.
I think I should not be encouraged to grow
tomatoes. Or, if I am, you should withhold
the heavy rains, the cold nights that come
so often here, while other regions get
twelve weeks of summer. All this
belongs to you: on the other hand,
I planted the seeds, I watched the first shoots
like wings tearing the soil, and it was my heart
broken by the blight, the black spot so quickly
multiplying in the rows. I doubt
you have a heart, in our understanding of
that term. You who do not discriminate
between the dead and the living, who are, in consequence,
immune to foreshadowing, you may not know
how much terror we bear, the spotted leaf,
the red leaves of the maple falling
even in August, in early darkness: I am responsible
for these vines.

from *The New Yorker*

Body Will

◊ ◊ ◊

My body to idiom and text   My flesh to pot,
along with some other distinctions   My limbs
out in reckless positions   My feet to the
six I'm underneath, inching east   My nerves
to impulse, their patient transmissions   My
back to the ground, to the track past the door
My spine in its hardcover volume   My bones to
their dry study   My face to what's in store
My chest to the treasury   My heart to both
change and rote   My blood, in circulation,
to the thirsty mare in its stream   My arches
and brows to rogues at a bridge where rich and
poor rendezvous   My nose in my business   My
mouth to the bottle   My tongue in its groove,
in the cheek of a twister   My palms to crossing
My hands to spring and horses, keeping up with
promises   My lips in your service   My heels
to flight and followers   My elbows to society
My eyes to apples, the teeth they're aligned
with, to retribution   My nails to the clincher
My neck to risk, to the forest trees lacing
land   My ears to debt and shot and splitting
My hair to fractures, to sensitive triggers

My mind to the reader   My head to its bed,
gray pillow of stone, to the strong in the wind
who make their way home.

from *ZYZZYVA*

JORIE GRAHAM

Manifest Destiny

◇   ◇   ◇

(Note: Rebbibia is the name of the women's jail in Rome)
(F. H. 1947–1990)

Northbound, on the way to the station, through the narrow
rutted
place in the patch of woods,
the dust from the car ahead rose up
into the wide still shafts of morning-light the trees let
through,
its revolutionary swirls uplifted in some kind of
cosmic merriment, up

all round the sleek whiskey-colored slice
of time
passing—though perfectly still to our eyes, passengers—
a blade of stillness, the intravenous access
of the unearthly
into this soil.
The dust rose into it. No, the dust

slapped round, falling, a thick curiosity, shabby but
extravagant, crazy pulverized soliloquy, furled up, feathery,
around the
metronome, raking, as if to transfuse itself onto what won't be
touched,
a thick precipitate, feudal, a glossary of possible entrances
replete

with every conceivable version of
change.
    Change! It seemed to almost screech as it rose again and
                                          again
out of our drought into the stiff and
    prosperous stillness—*change, change*—into, onto
that shaft driven in firm,

    steely backbone of the imperial
invisible.
    I watched the stationary golden avenue. At every curve
watched the dust
    thrown up like some mad prophet taking on
all the shapes, all the contortions of the
    human form—bent over, flayed, curled back

onto itself.
    It was hard not to see the grief in it, the
cowardice—
    this carnage of fictive
possibilities, this prolonged
    carnage.
The gold bars gleam.
    The money is put down on the gleaming platter.
Like an eyelid forced back down.
    And another bill, and another bill, down,—
onto the open hand, onto the open,—

    — how long till the blazing gaze is dulled, the wide
need, bristling with light,
    unwavering, shimmering with rightfulness, god,
so still!—
    and the dusty money coming down onto it.

We rose from the table having paid our bill.

    Rome stepped back all round us as we rose up

— colonnades, promenades, porticoes,
    shadows of warriors, lovers and the various queens of
heaven—

    arms raised holding the stone fruit, lips parted uttering the
stone word—stone child in the stone arms—stone

    sword held up into the stone
cry—.
    I look into the air
for your face—
    a fold in the invisible out of which features
slip—
    until you put it on again, there, in the dusty air, the
expression you wore, click,
    among the shadows of the sculptures in the

Vatican arcade—3 miles of corridor we hurry through
    to reach the reliquary before it shuts,
to see the Veronica,
    your hands pressed to the glass till the guard
speaks—
    and the eyes in brine,
and the index finger of Aquinas,
    and the burned head of Lawrence so black it seems
to face on all four

sides—then back out into the noon
    sun. *Rome.* And the word pulverizes. In the restaurant
you were gone so long I
    came to look for you.
Your face started up from the two arms below you—
    one holding the needle into the other—

white kiss on the brow of the forever waiting white maiden,
    forever and forever, forever and forever.
We paid up and left there too.
    The city even whiter now. White noise. White light.

Walking the back way we passed the length of Rebibbia.
Cooler down there. Riverside traffic above to the left.
   We were used to them, the women's shrieks—hanging their arms,
hundreds of them, out through the bars into the steamy
heat—pointing, cursing, all the fingers in the dark noonlight
       screaming down the stories—who was killed, why, where
the children are, will you take a message, I'd do it again,
   I'd do it to you, come on, let me give it to you—thousands
of white fingers all over the dark facade, no faces
                                    visible—just

listen, listen and I'll make you
       come they'd shriek, trellis of iron and white fleshgrowth,
3 blocks long this queen of the skies—huntress—no face—

   all stone and fingerclutch, white, raking the air.
You stood below looking up,
       the thing which is your laugh sucked up like a small down-
payment—so small—
       then taking my arm, hard, forced me to stand there
before them, below them—*here, do you want her, will she do* you
                                    screamed—
   thousands of fingers moving—*tell me, will she do*—

screech of muscle,
       throbbing facade,
how should we make her you screamed
       do her time, drunk too I thought, the clamp of your hand
hard on my upper arm,
       the light down harder on my face, something rising in me
                                    as they

screamed down give her to us, let us have her,
       their one scream going in through
the hold where your hand gripped, the narrow opening
       through which I knew
that you would not believe in life,
       that you would hand the piece you were holding back up,

the debt too heavy to carry,
    up to the balcony there, in full sun,

like a caress on the infinite
    this handing up of the full amount,
a handful of cloth, cash, skin—
    2:53 pm—Rome time—
in the marketplace now, in the arcade,
    arms waving the flies off
over the cut meats, beside the statue of Caesar—
    two dancers with a hat out for change—
the swallower of flames, the fabric merchant

    holding the star-spangled yardage out on her arms,
and singing the price out—loud, clear,
    —*what is love what is creation what is longing what
is a star*—
    behold I show you the last man—
the price rising up on the gold track of its note,
    the cloth on her arms lifting,

catching the light, dustmotes in the light,
    and the voice thrusting round it,
and the unalterable amount—
    high, hard, doth she and did she and shall she ever more—
sleeps she a thousand years and then and then—
    a motorcycle through it now then a dog—
the last man grows, lives longest,
    is ineradicable—blink—
"we have invented happiness" he says—
    meats sizzling on the silver spit,
price aloft,

    perfect price in the dusty air,
us swirling round its upwardmoving note,
    milling, taking this shape then that, hot wind,

until I have to turn to let her voice in,
    to feel the blue velveteen spangly brocade,
the invisible sum with its blazing zero ajar, there, midair—

    and something so quick darting through it—
what will my coin repair? what does my meaning mend?

    I pay her now. I pay her again. Again.
Gold open mouth hovering—no face.

    Until you're pulling me away. Saying *love*.
As if to find me with that.
    But I want to pay her again.
To keep the hole open.
    The zero. The gold lidless pupil.
She will not look away.
    Change change it shrieks   the last man blinks   we have invented,
                                        invented—

Oh why are you here on this earth, you—*you*—swarming, swirling,
    carrying valises, standing on line,
ready to change your name if need be—?

Poland of Death (IV)

◊   ◊   ◊

1.

It is the duty of every man,
And woman, to write the life of the mother.
But the life of the father is written by
The father alone.—Now he is of great size
In Poland of Death, and his garment is sewn
Of superior cloth. I came upon him down
An alley of that place, sitting on a wall,
At the intersection of two walls, looking wise:
Known there as Louis of Minneapolis,
The *maître à pensée* of the necropolis.
And his song was, "When the deep purple falls. . . ."

2.

As I came up, he cast me a sharp glance
And stopped short at the middle of the verse
("Sleepy garden walls . . .")—meaning, "This is
Your last chance to say something." "*Say* something!"
"How do you like my suit?" And so I say
To him, "You looked better naked and small."
And he says, "What's given here can never be
Refused, or lost. That's the rule. Take this nail!"

Then he started an old song I didn't like
At all. Something of the "matter of the race"—
At very least the long and sonorous breath

3.

Of a dark language.—O Poland of Death!
I asked a beggar-woman of the cemetery
What he sang, the young one smelling of sea
And milk who sweeps the sill. "Louis," she replies,
"Is a proud Jew now, dwelling among the dead,
A big Rabbi of rats dressed in a suit
That fits. A prince!" And then—before my eyes—
On the vapors of the universe—the head
Of Louis hung—like Brutus, the conspirator;
And its song poured back centuries of rain
From the Etruscan jar of an old man's voice

4.

Into the water-wells of the abyss:
"Now I know everything," it sang, "being in
The right place!—How did I get so wise?
When I proceeded Doctor of Philosophy
Torches smoked and flamed from every tower.
(Let the flame leap up, the heart ignite and burn!)
The celebrations of commencement were elaborate,
And I was clothed then, as you see me now,
In a suit that fits, sewn of superior cloth,
Invulnerable to the rust, the moth,
And the diurnal changes of the light

5.

In the air. My boy, the truth is great."
"Louis," I cried, "soon I am going to die.
The world is nearing its end. Say something
I can understand!" So he pulled out a beret
Of reddish brown, put it on his head, and smiled
Like a prince, as the woman said, or king—
(Of grave-diggers, as it seems, or wolves or Jews).
And I heard, then, the father calling to the son
And the son responding to the father from afar,
And the daughter to the mother, and the mother
To the children—voices like falling water,

6.

Or the shadow of swans, the sigh of the swan's feather:
"After a thousand years the Devil will be loosed
On a day, and in the morning of that day
This Louis will ride forth in his 1950
Chevrolet of prophecy—with feet, hands,
And four on the floor (Ezekiel I).
And the Rektor of the University
The Archbishop, the Lord Mayor and the General
Of Artillery, will applaud his face
And he will meet the host in the air,
Igniting the *auto-da-fé* of the sun."

7.

But all I understood, in fact, was the next phrase
On of the song he was singing as he sat
At the intersection (you will remember it)
Of two walls, "When the deep purple falls."
This time he got as far as the "nightingales."
Then stopped, and shouted, "This is the story

Of my life. I am the Professor now
Bigger than the Lord God. *He* was seduced
And made the world against His will—by art.
My son, I never married. I have no children.
I was smart. My father was a butcher, an empiricist

8.

Who knew the Law. (And that explains, in case
You want to *know*, why I hate cats! . . .)
When the end comes, like a dark wife at last,
It will be among the nightingales and rats
Of the necropolis, as the 'purple' falls
On Poland of Death." He turned his face, then,
And stopped his voice, never to speak again.
The Etruscan jar rang. I said to him: "Louis
I will sing you a new song." And the abyss
Supplied its words, "Halleluya!" *Praise
The Lord*. Then the beggar-woman of the cemetery

9.

Saw her chance, and gave the old man on the wall
A proper kiss. For what? For being wise,
And (after all) unmarried, and for dressing well.
Happy, happy Louis! The new song was this:
"Father, not father, *O roi magicien!*
Mother, not mother, O name of Beatrice!
Does the cloth forget the weaver, does the field
Of millet in its season no longer remember the sower,
Or the birds that feed on it honor in later summer
The labor that laid it down? O Yes! And the pot
The woman's hand who made it has forgot.

10.

How much less the mind, reading and running hard,
Touches the world. (O touch me, *roi thaumaturge!*)
Therefore, Louis of Minneapolis at ease upon a wall,
Sucking on a nail—the Jew in charge—
Demands a word when the deep purple falls.
What do I hear? An audible air of voices
Calling out and answering: *'Au revoir,
Ma femme chère,' 'Mon frère,' 'Ma soeur,' 'Mon père.'*
What do I see? Poland of Death! Louis driven out
(The Doctor in his garment of superior cloth)
Into the field behind the wall and shot!

11.

'What is the past?' 'What passes?' 'What is to come
When I have died?' . . . *What is to come?* No figure
Has it yet, no form.—Night falls in a room.
Someone in the dark is scratching with a nail:
The chronicler. Upon the road to the necropolis
Approaches always the chrome of battlecars,
Convertibles in columns like descended stars.
What is the past?—Night falls in a room. A king
Gives laws in the abyss on a drowned throne.
What passes?—The *auto-da-fé* of the sun.
What is the WORD? Halleluya. The Lord is ONE."

from *Tikkun*

Elysian Fields

◇ ◇ ◇

"Champs Elysées of Broadway" says the awning
of the café where, every Sunday morning,
young lawyers in old jeans ripped at the knees
do crosswords. Polyglot Lebanese
own it: they've taken on two more shopfronts
and run their banner down all three at once.
Four years ago, their sign, "Au Petit Beurre"
was so discreet, that, meeting someone there,
I'd tell her the street corner, not the name.
They were in the right place at the right time.
Meanwhile, the poor are trying hard enough.
Outside, on Broadway, people sell their stuff
laid out on blankets, cardboard cartons, towels.
A stout matron with lacquered auburn curls
circles the viridian throw rug
and painted plaster San Martín to hug
a thinner, darker woman, who hugs her
back volubly in Spanish—a neighbor,
I guess, and guess they still have houses.
The man with uncut, browned French paperbacks,
the man with two embroidered gypsy blouses
and three pilled pitiful pairs of plaid slacks
folded beside him on the pavement where
there was a Puerto Rican hardware store
that's been a vacant shopfront for two years
may not. There's a young couple down the block
from our corner: she's tall, gaunt, gangly, black;

he's short, quick, volatile, unshaven, white.
They set up shop dry mornings around eight.
I've seen him slap her face, jerking her thin
arm like a rag doll's—a dollar kept from him,
she moves too slow, whore, stupid bitch . . . "She's
my wife," he tells a passing man who stops
and watches. If anyone did call the cops
it would be to prevent them and their stacks
of old *Vogues* and outdated science texts
from blocking access to the "upscale bar"
where college boys get bellicose on beer.
 "Leave him," would I say? Does she have keys
to an apartment, to a room, a door
to close behind her? What we meant by "poor"
when I was twenty, was a tenement
with clanking pipes and roaches; what we meant
was up six flights of grimed, piss-pungent stairs,
four babies and a baby-faced welfare
worker forbidden to say "birth control."
I was almost her, on the payroll
of New York State Employment Services
—the East 14th Street Branch, whose task it was
to send day-workers, mostly black, to clean
other people's houses. Five-fifteen
and I walked east, walked south, walked up my four
flights. Poor was a neighborhood, was next door,
is still a door away. The door is mine.
Outside, the poor work Broadway in the rain.
The cappuccino drinkers watch them pass
under the awning from behind the glass.

from *The Paris Review*

DONALD HALL

Spring Glen Grammar School

◊   ◊   ◊

THAT

I remember the moment because I planned, at six in the first grade,
to remember the moment forever. For weeks we memorized the
     alphabet,
reciting it in unison singsong, copying it in block capitals
on paper with wide lines, responding to letters on flashcards—
but we learned no words.
                              Then we heard: "Tomorrow we start to read."
Miss Stephanie Ford wrote on the blackboard, in huge letters,
T H A T. "That," she said, pointing her wooden stick, "is 'that.' "

POLITICS

Each year began in September with a new room and a new teacher:
I started with Stephanie Ford, then Miss Flint, Miss Sudell
whom I loved, Miss Stroker, Miss Fehm, Miss Pikosky . . .
                                                  At assemblies
I was announcer. I was elected Class President in the eighth grade,
not because they liked me—it wasn't a popularity contest—
but because I was polite to grown-ups, spoke distinctly,
kept my shirt tucked in, and combed my hair: I was presidential.

THE BOX

Eight years of Spring Glen Grammar School. If I should live
to be eighty, this box would contain the tithe of everything.
In the glass case there's a rock garden with tiny snails, mosses,
infinitesimal houses, sidewalks, scissors and crayons, teachers,
and a model of Spring Glen Grammar School.

                                           See, the doors swing
open; see, small pupils gather around a boy in blue knickers.
The box is humid; it continues to continue: Nothing escapes.

from *The New Yorker*

Infidelities

◇ ◇ ◇

I

I read somewhere that every love
has its own government. Or was it
that every love has
the government it deserves?
What is ours?
The heat of August is thick,
an unwoven blanket of air,
damp, present and persistent.
Here, we two representatives
half-sleep some place half-known,
remembered only
in moments of utter distraction,
but never in despair.
Before we depart, gain again
our former lives, we might
for the sake of transition
gaze a few moments
at the adjacent apartment house at dusk,
each window a single friendly frame
of others nearly like us, caught
in a life carried on
without the negotiations of duplicity.
We take up the habit
of referring to others
in the third person once-removed,

while for us there's only
the everlasting present: we walk out
into the general evening and you say
it's like walking out
of a deeply engaging matinee:
so much sudden light,
so much going on,
so much of what came before
still residing in us.
Is the frantic siren
playing our song?
You nearly say what we're committed
to saying never, the understood unsaid—
even here there are laws and rights
to protect the guilty,
even if the jury's always in.
Our penalty,
with conviction or without:
life sentences,
back-to-back.

II

There's a gray cat who's not allowed into the house
where our cat for twenty years has been the one cat.

There's a storm working over the low mountains,
building with a stillness of air and light

over the nearest peaks. And soon the rain,
the full storm gets underway, thunder and light,

the passing thickness of air, the sudden rush
of wind, and the sheet of rain spraying the valley.

The gray cat presses against the door frame, and we
        sit
down to dinner, our cat in the third chair, the stew

done right and placed on the table, the wine poured.
The evening survives the storm and we walk out for a
        look

at what's left. A moon finally free, a hostage
sprung from a Jihad of clouds breaking up. The wet
        grass

regains its starch from this afternoon's wet heat,
and the gray cat emerges from under the porch steps,

dry but intense, charging our legs and getting over
in the language of cats her wish to enter our lives.

In the window, mirroring the table lamp, our cat,
shrewd, disappointed, and accusatory, studies us.

She's hurt and shows no apparent sympathy for a
        sister
left to the cold of the outside world. We're not
        surprised,

she's an indoor cat, her claws clipped, her movements
suited to the angles of furniture, the surface of rugs.

She will stand before her bowl of food and demand
        our best,
a gourmet cat when hungry: squab, fillet, hearts of
        chicken.

III

Adjoining suites in cities halfway round the world.
Flowers for your room or mine?—we are all of us
so thoughtful by distance, by way of longing
known only to those left what once was shared,
        shared
dailiness. The sun sets in Malaysia, comes up
in Malawi, sets again almost anywhere. There's local
        beer
in Srinagar, dangerous fish to consume at gold prices
in Tokyo, dishes spiced with ground cumin
along the North African coast—part of the
        experience.

Don't forget postcards: Etc., Love, . . .
Don't eat salads east of the Mediterranean;
in general, leave the uncooked to local consumption.
For the last night there's suddenly a balcony,
a table set for one, mirrored by an adjoining table,
set for one, a vase of flowers each, a flinty white
from Chablis, a napkin bleached and starched stiff.
        Two,
under whatever local weather can manage. To
        departure!
To one more long flight back. To the airline's pressed
        meat.
To the whimsy of airport control. To the profound
second-rate paperback novel whose hapless characters
in their tireless sprint around the track of love
will accompany you the full distance home.

IV

We talked in the oyster bars
and on the streets the homeless
entertained us, dancing or singing,

clowning for the homeowners, hats out,
hands out, moving.
                           Strolling
is what we do here, destination
left for later. And later we're somewhere dark,
the music higher, off the street,
an arena of candlelit tables, black leather
actors playing the role of waiters
and bad wine poured out of unmarked jugs
which we drink with impunity.

There are those listening to music,
those trading one practiced gesture for another.
Where do we go from here? The set's ended
and the food begins to arrive at the tables.

Back on the street it's late, dangerous
if you read the papers or listen to the cabbies.
There's a moon hung up there but it's soiled.
There are stars too somewhere, but hidden
behind this air, thick with accrual—of
everything about life in this town.
We can talk away by one body of water or another,
the evening's finished and we are like everything here,
strangers like everyone, without destination,
parting with nothing left to say.

V

There's a rich, humid park that carries on for acres.
It might be placed downtown, or simply midtown,
in a alrge, unknowable midwestern city, near a lake
whose native game fish draw those with time on their
          hands
from both East and West. Chartered boats, guides,
rented gear to fit the tall and short, the hip and
          guileless.

The two of us meet Wednesday afternoons there,
beneath hundred-year-old oaks that on sunny days
        toss shade
no less than a hundred feet. We meet there with
        blankets
and a bag of prepared lunch. The city sirens that
        work
the periphery of the park sing with care what we like
        to call,
simply, *our song*. We sip our wine, we mouth the
        lyrics

of what needs to be everlasting. We note what wants
        attention:
our careful dress, the casual play of hair and
        percentage
of color in the other's complexion, blood at the
        surface,
superior attention is how we begin to understand the
        face
looking back, filled with expression, looking for the
        necessary
translation, required understanding. On the sea

it's red sky at night, sailor's delight, simple directions.
Buoys: red right returning. Our damp hands, finally
        freed,
mean business if we allow the passing on of
        substance.
We'll look for signs deep in the agates of vision,
        peepholes
into the deep emotional stations we call our hearts.
Not even the storm forming overhead will drive us
        back.

Not even the inclement work of weather will defeat
    the good purpose
of this afternoon. A freight train pulls a hundred
    Chryslers
up the hill we've yet to coin a name for, claim as one
    more
possession, one more part of the memory—we with
    little else
than an afternoon to spare in the sparse post-storm
    light.
We want it this lingering way: constant renaming,
    constant return.

from *The Paris Review*

My Mother's Nipples

◇   ◇   ◇

They're where all displacement begins.
They bulldozed the upper meadow at Squaw Valley,
where horses from the stable, two chestnuts, one white,
grazed in the mist and the scent of wet grass on summer mornings
and moonrise threw the owl's shadow on voles and wood rats
crouched in the sage smell the earth gave back
with the day's heat to the night air,
and after they had gouged up the deep-rooted bunchgrass
and the wet alkali-scented earth had been pushed aside
or trucked someplace out of the way, they poured concrete
and laid road—pleasant scent of tar in the spring sun—
and after the framers began to pound nails
and the electricians and plumbers came around to talk specs
with the general contractor, someone put up a green sign
with alpine daisies on it that said Squaw Valley Meadows.

★

"He wanted to get out of his head," she said,
"so I told him to write about his mother's nipples."

★

The cosmopolitan's song on this subject:

Alors! les nipples de ma mère!

The romantic's song

What could be more fair
than les nipples de ma mère?

The utopian's song

I will freely share
les nipples de ma mère.

The philosopher's song

Here was always there
with les nipples de ma mère

The capitalist's song

Fifty cents a share

The saint's song

Lift your eyes in prayer

The misanthrope's song

I can scarcely bear

The melancholic's song

They were never there,
les nipples de ma mère.
They are not anywhere.

The indigenist's song

And so the boy they called Loves His Mother's Tits
Went into the mountains and fasted for three days
On the fourth he saw a redtailed hawk with broken wings

On the fifth a gored doe in a ravine, entrails
Spilled onto the rocks, eye looking up at him
From the twisted neck. All the sixth day he was dizzy
And his stomach hurt. On the seventh he made three deep cuts
In the meat of his palm. He entered the pain at noon
And an eagle came to him crying three times like the mewling
A doe makes planting her hooves in the soft duff for mating
And he went home and they called him Eagle Three Times after that.

The regionalist's song

Los Pechos.
Rolling oak woodland between Sierra pines
and the simmering valley.

★

It was when he was asked to write about his mother's nipples
that Goethe made the famous observation
that all poems are occasional poems.

★

Pink, of course, soft; a girl's
She wore white muslin tennis outfits
in the style Helen Wills made fashionable.
Trim athletic swimsuits.
A small person, compact body. In the photographs
she's on the beach, standing straight,
hands on hips, grinning,
eyes desperate even then.

★

Mothers in the nineteen forties didn't nurse.
I never saw her naked. Oh! yes, I did,
once, but I can't remember. I remember
not wanting to.

Two memories. My mother had been drinking for several days, and I had thought dinner would be cancelled, so I wouldn't get to watch The Lone Ranger on my aunt's and uncle's television set. But we went to dinner and my aunt with her high-pitched voice took the high-minded tone that she took in my mother's presence. She had put out hard candies in little cut glass dishes as she always did, and we ate dinner, at which water was served to the grown-ups, and no one spoke except my uncle who teased us in his English accent. A tall man. He used to pat me on the head too hard and say, "Robert of Sicily, brother of the Pope Urbane." And after dinner when the television was turned on in the immaculate living room and Silver was running across the snowy screen, his mane shuddering from the speed, the doorbell rang. It was two men in white coats and my mother bolted from the table into the kitchen and out the back door. The men went in after her. The back stairs led into a sort of well between the two houses, and when I went into the kitchen I could hear her screaming, "No! no!", the sound echoing and re-echoing among the houses. Recently I asked my older brother if this ever happened.

Some years later. I am perhaps ten, eleven. We are visiting my mother on the park-like grounds of the State Hospital in the Napa Valley. It is Sunday again. Green lawns, the heavy sweet scent of mock orange. Many of the patients are walking, alone or with their families, on the paths. One man seemed to be giving speeches to a tree. I had asked my grandmother why, if my mother had a drink-ing problem, that's the phrase I had been taught to use, why she was locked up with crazy people. It was a question I could have asked my father, but I understood that his answer would not be dependable. My grandmother said, with force, she had small red curls on her forehead, dressed with great style, you had better ask your father that. Then she thought better of it, and said They have a treatment program, dear, maybe it will help. I tried out that phrase, treatment program. My mother was sitting on a bench. She looked immensely sad, seemed to have shrunk. Her hair was pulled across her forehead and secured with a white beret, like Teresa Wright in the movies. At first my brother and I just sat next to her on the bench and cried. My father held my sister's hand. My grandmother and grandfather stood to one side, a separate group, and watched. Later, while they talked, I studied a middle-aged woman sitting on the next bench talking to herself in a foreign language. She was wearing a floral print dress and she spoke almost in a whisper but with passion, looking around from time to time, quick little furtive resentful glances. She was so careless of herself that I could see her breast, the brown nipple, when she leaned forward. I didn't want to look, and looked, and looked away.

*

Hot Sierra morning.
Brenda working in another room.
Rumble of heavy equipment in the meadow,
bird squall, Steller's jay, and then
the piercing three-note whistle of a robin.
They're mating now. Otherwise they're mute.
Mother-ing. Or mother-song.
Mother-song-song-song.

*

We used to laugh, my brother and I in college,
about the chocolate cake. Tears in our eyes laughing.
In grammar school, whenever she'd start to drink,
she panicked and made amends by baking chocolate cake.
And, of course, when we got home, we'd smell the strong,
    sweet smell
of the absolute darkness of chocolate,
and be too sick to eat it.

*

The first girl's breasts I saw
were the Chevie dealer's daughter Linda Hen's.
Pale in the moonlight. Little nubbins, pink-nosed.
I can still hear the slow sound of the surf
of my breath drawing in. I think I almost fainted.

★

Twin fonts of mercy, they used to say of the Virgin's breasts
in the old liturgy the Irish priests
could never quite handle, it being a form of bodily reference,
springs of grace, freshets
of lovingkindness. If I remember correctly,
there are baroque poems in this spirit
in which each of Christ's wounds is a nipple.
Drink and live: this is the son's blood.

★

Dried figs, candied roses.

What is one to say of the nipples of old women
who would, after all, find the subject
unseemly.

Yesterday I ran along the edge of the meadow in the heat
of late afternoon. So many wildflowers
tangled in the grass. So many grasses—
reedgrass and bentgrass and timothy, little quaking grass,
dogtail, brome—the seeds flaring from the stalks
in tight chevrons of green and purple-green
but loosening.

I said to myself:
some things do not blossom in this life.

I said: what we've lost is a story
and what we've never had
a song.

When my father died, I was curious to see in what ratio she would
feel relieved and lost. All during the days of his dying, she stood
by his bed talking to whichever of her children was present about

the food in the cafeteria or the native state of the nurses—"She's from Portland, isn't that interesting? Your aunt Nell lived in Portland when Owen was working for the Fisheries."—and turn occasionally to my father who was half-conscious, his eyes a morphine cloud, and say, in a sort of baby talk, "It's all right, dear. It's all right." And after he died, she was dazed, and clearly did not know herself whether she felt relieved or lost, and I felt sorry for her that she had no habit and so no means of self-knowing. She was waiting for us to leave so she could start drinking. Only once was she suddenly alert. When the young man from the undertaker's came and explained that she would need a copy of her marriage license in order to do something about the insurance and pensions, she looked briefly alive, anxious, and I realized that, though she rarely told the truth, she was a very poor dissembler. Now her eyes were a young girl's. What, she asked, if someone just couldn't turn up a marriage license; it seemed such a detail, there must be cases. I could see that she was trying out avenues of escape, and I was thinking, now what? They were never married? That would be funny somehow. I told her not to worry. I'd locate it. She considered this and said it would be fine. I could see she had made some decision, and then she grew indefinite again.

So, back in California, it was with some interest that I retraced the drive from San Francisco to Santa Rosa which my parents made in 1939, when according to my mother's story—it was the first account of it I'd ever heard—she and my father had eloped. The Sonoma County Office of Records was in a pink cinderblock building landscaped with reptilian pink oleanders which were still blooming in the Indian summer heat. It would have been raining when my parents drove that road in an old (I imagined) cream-colored Packard convertible I had seen one photo of. I asked the woman at the desk for the marriage certificate for February 1939. I wondered what the surprise was going to be, and it was a small one. No problem, Mrs. Minh said. But you had the date wrong, so it took me a while to find it. It was October, not February. Driving back to San Francisco, I had time to review this information. My brother was born in December 1939. Hard to see that it meant anything except that my father had tried very hard to avoid his fate. I felt so sorry for them. That they thought it was worth keeping a secret. Or, more likely, that their life together began in a negotiation too painful to be referred to again. That my mother had, with a certain fatality, let me pick up the license, so her first son would not know the circumstance of his conception. I felt sorry for her shame, for my father's panic. It finished off my dim wish that there had been an early romantic or ecstatic time in their lives, a blossoming, brief as a northern summer maybe, but a blossoming.

What we've never had is a song
and what we've really had is a song.

Sweet smell of timothy in the meadow.
Clouds massing east above the ridge in a sky
as blue as the mountain lakes,
so there are places on this earth clear all the way up
and all the way down
and in between a various blossoming,
the many seed shapes of the many things
finding their way into flower or not,
that the wind scatters.

There are all kinds of emptiness and fullness
that sing and do not sing.

I said: you are her singing.

She had passed out in a park. I came home from school and she was gone. I don't know what instinct sent me there. I suppose it was the only place I could think of where someone might hide. It was a grassy hillside lawn. She had passed out under an orange tree, curled up. Her face, flushed, eyelids swollen, was a ruin. Though I needed urgently to know whatever was in it, I could hardly bear to look. When I couldn't wake her, I decided to sit with her until she woke up. I must have been ten years old: I suppose I wanted for us to look like a son and mother who had been picnicking, like a mother who had fallen asleep in the warm light and scent of orange blossoms and a boy who was sitting beside her daydreaming, not thinking about anything in particular.

You are not her singing, though she is what's
broken in a song.
She is its silences.

She may be its silences.

Hawk drifting in the blue air,
grey of the granite ridges,
incense cedars, pines.

I tried to think of some place on earth she loved.

I remember she only ever spoke happily
of high school.

from *Michigan Quarterly Review*

St. Luke Painting the Virgin

◇　◇　◇

St. Luke's eyes are steady on the babe.
I, insufficiently transfixed,
Am led inexorably beyond
Van der Weyden's (you call him "Roger,"
Just as you ought)—beyond the window
Roger has set behind radiant
St. Luke, peaceful knower, to gardens,
And beyond them
　　　　　　　　to find in the clear
Distance the delicate city street
Where the figures of humanity
Consult the ground, their eyes helplessly
On the details of history that
Hold them there in the street as the laws
Of perspective, not imperfectly,
Hold the infant before the St.'s eyes.

It is the beauty of these figures
As background, as reinterpreted
Landscape I cry for; to be landscape
Is not to be at the center, not
The first thing the painter, seizing his
Focus, illuminated, and what
Are we, unilluminated? What,
To go on, is illumination
For? In the painting, for instance,
The atrocity is not in fact

Visible on the streets but in the eyes
Of the painter—St. Luke. The painter,
Gazing only on the bright infant,
Instead of out the window, reaches
A conclusion not plainly implied
In infant glee. Yet St. Luke's face is plainly
Illuminated by what he sees
Directly before him, while I look
Over Roger's shoulder and out the
Window. And weep, to see the city
So delicate and outside, though
I grant the mistake, the mistake of
Weeping, that is, when perhaps I could
Move subtly into the paint and stand
Behind St. Luke. He looks calm enough.
But I, seeing what he sees, would have
No thought of Fridays, or windows, or

Outsides of any sort; this is
The essential weakness of eyes like
Mine, to see, faced with a divine light,
Nothing but divine light, which is why
Landscapes, or whatever you paint
Beyond the garden, become so central,
Not to the conception, which is all
Complete in what the St. sees, but
To the training of the eye that is,
After all, an action of painting

And illuminations. There are those
That descend to the street while the bright
Neon sign above the square that says
True Cigarets glows undiminished
As the hosts of heaven. In Boston,
Standing before this painting I thought,
Even as I was transported, of
Streets in general, the subway ride home,

And the expanse of walks, all crowded,
That lay between you and me at that
Moment. I thought, in short, of you. We

Have Roger to thank for this. With just
The Infant before me I might have
Stepped out of all those streets directly
Into the light—only in my mind,
Of course, thus forgetting the way

Home. As it was I found my way through
The shadows and arrived in your arms
Only slightly bruised, and all because
Roger kindly refrained from making
A portrait of Christ in unrelieved
Brilliance. Light is light. We are guided,
Sometimes, more easily by the faint
Revelations in the shapes shadows
Suggest than by the blank expanses
On the faces of stars. I find some
Guidance, anyway, in my dark fears
Of what lurks in the streets and come to
See the light more clearly because I
Have missed it so many times, many
Hours. Gaze at the ground, then look up,
Is my advice, and see light, at last,
As precious because we find it
In the darkness outside a garden
Between the light and the world.

from *Raritan*

JUAN FELIPE HERRERA

Iowa Blues Bar Spiritual

◊   ◊   ◊

Little Tokyo bar—

ladies night, smoky gauze balcony, whispering. Tommy Becker,
makes up words to *La Bamba*—request by "Hard Jackson,"

mechanic on the left side of Paulie, Oldies dancer, glowing
with everything inside of her, shattered remembrances, healed

in lavender nail polish, the jagged finger nail tapping. So
play it hard above this floor, this velvet desert. I want

the Titian ochre yeast of winter, keyboard man, fix your eyes
on my eyes and tell me handsome, how long will I live?

How many double fisted desires, crushed letters, will I lift
in this terrain? And this rumbling sleeve, this ironed flint

of inquisitions and imaginary executors, where shall I strike,
what proud stones? Will this fauna open for me, ever, this fuzz

anointed beak inside the bartender's mirrors, etched doves,
a cautious spiral Harley tank, hissing, this Indian bead choker

on Rita's neck? How long shall we remain as wavy reflections,
imitators of our own jacket's frown? Who shall awaken first?

Margo Fitzer, the waitress? I will say, Queen Margo, sing to me
stoic priestess of slavering hearts, three faint lines creased

on your satin belly, toss our planet onto your umber lacquer tray,
too empty now; make the earth spin its dog rhapsody, erotic

through this silvery offramp and flake, unfurl. We tumble across
this raceway in honey glazed traces, our arms ahead, the hands

flying to Ricky's Ice cream parlour, outside. I want to own one
someday, maybe on Thirty Second Street. You will see me

in my gelled waved hair, my busy wrists—so fast, a clown's
resolute gloves, dipping faster than finger painting—except

I'd be stirring milk and the light chocolate foam of love, churning,
burning this sweet spirit, more uncertain, than the celestial

sheaths above the prairie frost. See the boy coming, they chide,
leaning, how he crosses his legs, his eyes dreaming, sideburns

just shaved clean. He weighs the sour slate on his father's breath;
perfume, fortune, cards left on the bleeding table. Milo Wilkens,
        drummer

at the curve, strokes his nipples with his arms as he hits the high hat.
Somewhere in the back rooms, I know, a shrine, orange sponge
        cushions,

two toilets and a wire wound wicker box, to leave flowers, occasional
offerings by the Johnson County dudes, detasslers in jersey ties.

Talk no more, enjoy. Darling singer, let your starry blouse sway me,
steal this fresh peach halve from its amber juice; I want the moon

in this nectar, too. The flashing cymbals, feverish. Who can strike
a votive candle, love, or sleep in this electronic night? Just listen

to the two-part harmony, laughter, peeling beyond the cemetery,
    beyond
the Iowa river—where the spike hat rooster bristles his tiny ears,

bows his head and sips from the dark cannister under the carved
    pearlstone.
And then, returns. Let us drink, salute the bright spokes of meal,
    the dying

wands of river blossoms, grandmother's sacred hair; listen, her soprano
owl, her bluish melody, so thin. Another glass please, we shall dance

once again, our eyebrows smearing against each other's cheekbones,
    loud
with a Midwest sweat, a cantata from the cross-hatch amp, click it.

Click it, for wild kind rain, forgiving seasons, for the blushed bread
of our shoulders and thighs, this night, everyone is here. Even Jeff
    Yoder

came all the way from Illinois, to fill a bucket with passion, ruffled,
thick. O Sax player with a jail needle tattoo, leap onto this wet
    pavement,

call my lonesome tempest heart, its buried mother's kiss, bless us
in staccato, with quivers of Oak branch greenness and sparrow
    longings

riff over this brutal sky, give us your bell filled, conjure your topic,
our lover's breath. Blues bar dancers, jangling gold popcorn, chord
    makers,

opal-eyed Suzie in a flannel shirt; we beckon the spark, the flaring,
this lost body to live.

from *New England Review*

Man on a Fire Escape

◇ ◇ ◇

He couldn't remember what propelled him
out of the bedroom window onto the fire escape
of his fifth-floor walkup on the river,

so that he could see, as if for the first time,
sunset settling down on the dazed cityscape
and tugboats pulling barges up the river.

There were barred windows glaring at him
from the other side of the street
while the sun deepened into a smoky flare

that scalded the clouds gold-vermillion.
It was just an ordinary autumn twilight—
the kind he had witnessed often before—

but then the day brightened almost unnaturally
into a rusting, burnished, purplish-red haze
and everything burst into flame;

the factories pouring smoke into the sky,
the trees and shrubs, the shadows,
of pedestrians scorched and rushing home. . . .

There were storefronts going blind and cars
burning on the parkway and steel girders
collapsing into the polluted waves.

Even the latticed fretwork of stairs
where he was standing, even the first stars
climbing out of their sunlit graves

were branded and lifted up, consumed by fire.
It was like watching the start of Armageddon,
like seeing his mother dipped in flame. . . .

And then he closed his eyes and it was over.
Just like that. When he opened them again
the world had reassembled beyond harm.

So where had he crossed to? Nowhere.
And what had he seen? Nothing. No foghorns
called out to each other, as if in a dream,

and no moon rose over the dark river
like a warning—icy, long forgotten—
while he turned back to an empty room.

from *The New Yorker*

Identities

◊ ◊ ◊

One searches roads receding, endlessly receding, receding.
The other opens all the doors with the same key. Simple.

One's quick to wrath, the wronged, the righteous, the wroth
    kettledrum.
The other loafs by the river, idles and jiggles his line.

One conspires against statues on stilts, in his pocket
The plot that dooms the city. The other's a *good* son.

One proclaims he aims to put the first aardvark in space.
The other patiently toils to make saddles for horseless headmen.

One exults as he flexes the glees of his body, up-down, up-down.
The other's hawk-kite would sail, would soar—who has tied it
    to carrion and bones?

One's a Tom Fool about money—those are his pockets, those with
    the holes.
At his touch, gold reverts to the base living substance.

The other's a genius, his holdings increase by binary fission—
Ownings beget their own earnings, dividend without end.

One clasps in a bundle and keens for the broken ten laws.
The other scratches in Ogham the covenant of a moral pagan.

One with alacrity answers to '121-45-3628?'—'Yes, *sir!*'
    The other
Bends his knee, doffs cap to no man living or dead. One

Does all his doings as ordained by diskette or disc.
The other draws his dreams through the eye of the moon.

from *Boulevard*

Days of Autumn

◇   ◇   ◇

1

Dusty leaves cast their shadows, and the bee,
That ancient prophetess, now wordlessly
      Buzzing of the wide wilderness, believes
Those shadows cast by what will come to be.

2

The full, ripe silence where the grain was sown
The lingering sigh of tall grass lately mown,
      Rise from these tedious, ordinary fields:
Don't draw on outline, but take note of tone.

3

The day of the long days has shed its noon,
Lain nakedly, and now awaits the moon,
      Donning the orange veil that sunset draws
Across what will be long ago too soon.

4

August remembered autumn, but not old
December, as its shortening days unrolled.
    Heat waved away, in summary dismissal
The winter's now-long-buried pot of cold.

5

Fields; the late harvest standing still in sheaves:
Is it the rising of the wind that grieves
    My forest self, *mon* moi *longue d'Octobre*
Who sang before the falling of the leaves?

6

Cadences of familiar songs Can lie
In hiding here Where fields and open sky
    Declaim In prose, unchanted, clear, The texts
Left high and dry When the fall wind swept by.

7

"*Ist Sommer? Sommer* war," wrote Paul Celan.
Imperfect autumn lingers, and so on
    And so forth while we pause as the last song
Of one lost summer swims by like a swan.

8

At length, the hill of thought was undermined
By pain, tunneling through its hard and blind
    Rock, into which runs our advancing train,
Leaving the plain of fancies far behind.

9

Ah, for her I lost! for me whom I gave
Away to nothing! for all I could not save!
    The raving wind disperses in the oaks.
Light grieving slumps into a heavy grave.

10

No nova flaring in November, less
And less renewal as the trees undress:
    We shiver down past mere noon and its non-
Age, and its hopeless whiffs of agelessness.

11

Blood's shadow lay beneath the light green shade
The chestnut branches by the meadow made.
    The field of beets became a battlefield,
The plough's fair share fell to another blade.

12

Autumn's brood stripped by late November's rude
Whips, our decaying health last year renewed
    Our well-known bodies' growing oddness, the
Stupidity of our decrepitude.

13

Above my dimmed eyes the barn owl, below
The shivering mouse, and then—and so we go.
    The dark point of this nocturne's both what I
Believe I see and what I know I know.

14

It was the gray sidewalks which taught my feet
The truth of their particular concrete:
    All? not this general Being of the land;
The *Way?* not through the fields, but up the street.

15

The years of childhood days—extended fears,
Joys and anticipations: time and tears
    Contract their terms, which, in the Psalmist's phrase,
Have withered to the brief days of our years.

16

That bright, young person that I was, all prim
Exuberance, safe wonder, bridled vim:
    Ingrate! He never gave a damn for me.
I weep for what I could have done for him.

17

Shining in sunlight through the winter trees
These little brooks appear now as they freeze,
    At liberty to glitter, at long last
Recovered from fluidity's disease.

January. Epipromethean, or
Just plain two-faced? Here standing at the door
    Of the year, staring both in and out, he knows
What lies before him is what has gone before.

from *Grand Street*

Like Most Revelations

◊   ◊   ◊

after Morris Louis

It is the movement that incites the form,
discovered as a downward rapture—yes,
it is the movement that delights the form,
sustained by its own velocity. And yet

it is the movement that delays the form
while darkness slows and encumbers; in fact
it is the movement that betrays the form,
baffled in such toils of ease, until

it is the movement that deceives the form,
beguiling our attention—we supposed
it is the movement that achieves the form.
Were we mistaken? What does it matter if

it is the movement that negates the form?
Even though we give (give up) ourselves
to this mortal process of continuing,
it is the movement that creates the form.

From *The Boston Phoenix*

LYNDA HULL

Lost Fugue for Chet

◇ ◇ ◇

Chet Baker, Amsterdam, 1988

A single spot slides the trumpet's flare then stops
    at that face, the extraordinary ruins thumb-marked
with the hollows of heroin, the rest chiaroscuroed.
    Amsterdam, the final gig, canals & countless

stone bridges arc, glimmered in lamps. Later this week
    his Badlands face, handsome in a print from thirty
years ago, will follow me from the obituary page
    insistent as windblown papers by the black cathedral

of Saint Nicholas standing closed today: pigeon shit
    & feathers, posters swathing tarnished doors, a litter
of syringes. Junkies cloud the gutted railway station blocks
    & dealers from doorways call *coca, heroina*, some throaty

foaming harmony. A measured inhalation, again
    the sweet embouchure, metallic, wet stem. Ghostly,
the horn's improvisations purl & murmur
    the narrow *strasses* of *Rosse Buurt*, the district rife

with purse-snatchers, women alluring, desolate, poised
    in blue windows, Michelangelo boys, hair spilling
fluent running chords, mares' tails in the sky green
    & violet. So easy to get lost, these cavernous

brown cafés. Amsterdam, & its spectral fogs, its
    softly shining tugboats. He builds once more
the dense harmonic structure, the gabled houses.
    Let's get lost. Why court the brink & then step back?

After surviving, what arrives? So what's the point
    when there are so many women, creamy callas with single
furled petals turning in & in upon themselves
    like variations, nights when the horn's coming

genius riffs, metal & spit, that rich consuming rush
    of good dope, a brief languor burnishing
the groin, better than any sex. Fuck Death.
    In the audience, there's always this gaunt man, cigarette

in hand, black Maserati at the curb, waiting,
    the fast ride through mountain passes, descending with
no rails between asphalt & precipice. Inside, magnetic
    whispering *take me there, take me.* April, the lindens

& horse chestnuts flowering, cold white blossoms
    on the canal. He's lost as he hears those inner voicings,
a slurred veneer of chords, molten, fingering
    articulate. His glance below Dutch headlines, the fall

"accidental" from a hotel sill. Too loaded. What do you do
    at the brink? Stepping back in time, I can only
imagine the last hit, lilies insinuating themselves
    up your arms, leaves around your face, one hand vanishing

sabled to shadow. The newsprint photo & I'm trying
    to recall names, songs, the sinuous figures, but facts
don't matter, what counts is out of pained dissonance,
    the sick vivid green of backstage bathrooms, out of

broken rhythms—and I've never forgotten, never—
   this is the tied-off vein, this is 3 a.m. terror
thrumming, this is the carnation of blood clouding
   the syringe, you shaped *summer rains across the quays*

of Paris, flame suffusing jade against a girl's
   dark ear. From the trumpet, pawned, redeemed, pawned again
you formed one wrenching blue arrangement, a phrase endlessly
   complicated as that twilit dive through smoke, applause,

the pale haunted rooms. Cold chestnuts flowering April
   & you're falling from heaven in a shower of eighth notes
to the cobbled street below & foaming dappled horses
   plunge beneath the still green waters of the Grand Canal.

from *The Kenyon Review*

LAWRENCE JOSEPH

Some Sort of Chronicler I Am

◇ ◇ ◇

Some sort of chronicler I am, mixing
perceptions and emotional digressions,

choler, melancholy, a sanguine view.
Through a transparent eye, the need, sometimes

to see everything simultaneously
—strange need to confront everyone

with equal respect. Although the citizen
across the aisle on the Number Three

subway doesn't appreciate my respect.
Look at his eyes—both of them popping

from injections of essence of poppy;
listen to his voice bordering on a shrill.

His declaration: he's a victim of acquired
immune deficiency syndrome. His addiction

he acquired during the Indo-Chinese war.
Named "underclass" by the Department of Labor

—he's underclass, all right: no class
if you're perpetually diseased and poor.

Named "blessed" by one of our Parnassians
known to effect the egotistical sublime

—blessed, indeed; he's definitely blessed.
His wounds open, here, on the surface:

you might say he's shrieking his stigmata.
I know—you'd prefer I change the subject.

(I know how to change the subject.)
Battery Park's atmosphere changes

mists in which two children play and scratch
like a couple of kittens until the green

layers of light cover them completely,
a sense of anguished fulfillment arising

without me, beauty needled into awareness
without me, beauty always present within

what happened that instant her silhouette
moved across the wall, magnified sounds

her blouse made scraped against her skin
—workers, boarded storefronts, limousines

with tinted windows, windows with iron bars,
lace-patterned legs, someone without legs,

merged within the metathetical imagination
we're all part of, no matter how personal

we think we are. Has anyone considered
during the depression of 1921

Carlos Williams felt a physician's pain,
vowed to maintain the most compressed

expression of perceptions and ardors
—intrinsic, undulant, physical movement—

revealed in the speech he heard around him
(dynamization of emotions into imagined

form as a reality in itself).
Wallace Stevens—remember his work

covered high-risk losses—knowingly chose
during the bank closings of early '33

to suspend his grief between social planes
he'd transpose into thoughts, figures, colors

—you don't think he saw the woman beneath
golden clouds tortured by destitution,

fear too naked for her own shadow's shape?
In 1944, an Alsatian who composed

poems both in French and German, exiled
for fear of death in a state-created camp—

his eye-structure, by law, defined "Jewish"—
sensed the gist. Diagnosed with leukemia,

Yvan Goll gave the name Lackawanna
Manahatta to our metropolis—Manahatta

locked in Judgment's pregnant days, he sang,
Lackawanna of pregnant nights and sulphurous

pheasant mortality riddled with light
lying dormant in a shock of blond hair

half made of telephones, half made of tears.
The heavy changes of the light—I know.

Faint silver of new moon and distant Mars
glow through to Lackawanna Manahatta.

Above a street in the lower Nineties
several leaves from an old ginkgo tree

twist through blackish red on golden air
outside a fashionable bistro where a man

with medals worn across a tailor-cut suit
chides a becoming woman half his age.

"From now on, my dear," he says with authority,
"from now on it's every man for himself."

from *The Kenyon Review*

The Man on the Hotel Room Bed

◇ ◇ ◇

He shifts on the bed carefully, so as
not to press through the first layer
into the second, which is permanently sore.
For him sleep means lying as still as possible
for as long as possible thinking the worst.
Nor does it help to outlast the night—
in seconds after the light comes
the inner darkness falls over everything.
He wonders if the left hand of the woman
in the print hanging in the dark above the bed,
who sits half turned away, her right hand
clutching her face, lies empty,
or does it move in the hair of a man
who dies, or perhaps died long ago
and sometimes comes and puts his head in her lap,
and goes again and lies under a sign
in a field filled nearly up to the roots
that hold down the hardly ever trampled grass
with mortals, the once-lovers. He goes over
the mathematics of lying awake all night alone
in a strange room: still the equations require
multiplication, by fear, of what is,
to the power of desire. He feels around—
no pillow next to his, no depression
in the pillow, no head in the depression.

Love is the religion that bereaves the bereft.
No doubt his mother's arms still waver up
somewhere reaching for him; and perhaps
his father's are now ready to gather him
there where peace and death dangerously mingle.
But the arms of prayer, which pressed his chest
in childhood—long ago, he himself, in the name of truth,
let them go slack. He lies face-down,
like something washed up. Out the window
first light pinks the glass building across the street.
In the religion of love to pray is to pass,
by a shining word, into the inner chamber
of the other. It is to ask the father and mother
to return and be forgiven. But in this religion
not everyone can pray, least of all
a man lying alone to avoid being abandoned,
who wants to die to escape the meeting with death.
The final second strikes. On the glass wall
the daylight grows so bright the man sees
the next darkness already forming inside it.

from *The Ohio Review*

Twelve O'Clock

◊ ◊ ◊

At seventeen I've come to read a poem
At Princeton. Now my young hosts inquire
If I would like to meet Professor Einstein.
But I'm too conscious I have nothing to say
To interest him, the genius fled from Germany just in time.
"Just tell me where I can look at him," I reply.

Mother had scientific training. I did not;
She loved that line of Meredith's about
The army of unalterable law.
God was made manifest to her in what she saw
As the supreme order of the skies.
We lay in the meadow side by side, long summer nights

As she named the stars with awe.
But I saw nothing that was rank on rank,
Heard nothing of the music of the spheres,
But in the bliss of meadow silences
Lying on insects we had mashed without intent,
Found overhead a beautiful and terrifying mess,

Especially in August, when the meteors whizzed and zoomed,
Echoed, in little, by the fireflies in the grass.
Although, small hypocrite, I was seeming to assent,
I was dead certain that uncertainty
Governed the universe, and everything else,
Including Mother's temperament.

A few years earlier, when I was four,
Mother and Father hushed before the Atwater-Kent
As a small voice making ugly noises through the static
Spoke from the grille, church-window-shaped, to them:
"Listen, darling, and remember always;
It's Doctor Einstein broadcasting from Switzerland."

I said, "So what?" This was repeated as a witticism
By my doting parents. I was dumb and mortified.
So when I'm asked if I would like to speak to Einstein
I say I only want to look at him.
"Each day in the library, right at twelve,
Einstein comes out for lunch." So I am posted.

At the precise stroke of noon the sun sends one clear ray
Into the center aisle: He just appears,
Baggy-kneed, sockless, slippered, with
The famous ravelling grey sweater;
Clutching a jumble of papers in one hand
And in the other his brown sack of sandwiches.

The ray haloes his head! Blake's vision of God,
Unmuscular, serene, except for the electric hair.
In that flicker of a second our smiles meet:
Vast genius and vast ignorance conjoined;
He fixed, I fluid, in a complicit yet
Impersonal interest. He dematerialized and I left, content.

It was December sixth, exactly when,
Just hours before the Japanese attack
The Office of Scientific R & D
Began "its hugely expanded program of research
Into nuclear weaponry"—racing the Germans who, they feared,
Were far ahead. In fact, they weren't.

Next night, the coach to school; the train, *Express*,
Instead pulls into every hamlet: grim young men
Swarm the platforms, going to enlist.

I see their faces in the sallow light
As the train jolts, then starts up again,
Reaching Penn Station hours after midnight.

At dinner in New York in '44, I hear the name
Of Heisenberg: Someone remarked, "I wonder where he is,
The most dangerous man alive. I hope we get to him in time."
Heisenberg. I kept the name. Were the Germans, still,
Or the Russians, yet, a threat? Uncertainty. . . .
But I felt a thrill of apprehension: Genius struck again.

It is the stroke of twelve—and I suppose
The ray that haloes Einstein haloes me:
White-blonde hair to my waist, almost six feet tall,
In my best and only suit. Why cavil?—I am beautiful!
We smile—but it has taken all these years to realize
That when I looked at Einstein he saw me.

At last that May when Germany collapsed
The British kidnapped Heisenberg from France
Where he and colleagues sat in a special transit camp
Named "Dustbin", to save them from a threat they never knew:
A mad American general thought to solve
The post-war nuclear problem by having them all shot.

Some boys in pristine uniforms crowd the car
(West Pointers fleeing from a weekend dance?),
Youth's ambiguities resolved in a single action.
I still see their faces in the yellow light
As the train jolts, then starts up again,
So many destined never to be men.

In Cambridge the Germans visited old friends
Kept apart by war: Austrians, English, Danes,
"In a happy reunion at Farm Hall."
But then the giant fist struck—in the still
Center of chaos, noise unimaginable, we thought we heard
The awful cry of God.

Hiroshima. Heisenberg at first refused
To believe it, till the evening news confirmed
That their work had lead to Hiroshima's 100,000 dead.
"Worst hit of us all," said Heisenberg, "was Otto Hahn,"
Who discovered uranium fission. "Hahn withdrew to his room,
And we feared that he might do himself some harm."

It is exactly noon, and Doctor Einstein
Is an ancient drawing of the sun.
Simple as a saint emerging from his cell
Dazed by his own light. I think of Giotto, Chaucer,
All good and moral medieval men
In—yet removed from—their historic time.

The week before we heard of Heisenberg
My parents and I are chatting on the train
From Washington. A grey-haired handsome man
Listens with open interest, then inquires
If he might join us. We were such a fascinating family!
"Oh yes," we chorus, "sit with us!"

Penn Station near at hand, we asked his name.
E. O. Lawrence, he replied, and produced his card.
I'd never heard of him, but on an impulse asked,
"What is all this about the harnessing
Of the sun's rays? Should we be frightened?"
He smiled. "My dear, there's nothing in it."

So, reassured, we said goodbyes,
And spoke of him in coming years, that lovely man.
Of course we found out who he was and what he did,
At least as much as we could comprehend.
Now I am living in the Berkeley hills,
In walking distance of the Lawrence lab.

Here where Doctor Lawrence built the cyclotron,
It's noon: the anniversary of Hiroshima:
Everywhere, all over Japan

And Germany, people are lighting candles.
It's dark in Germany and Japan, on different days,
But here in Berkeley it is twelve o'clock.

I stand in the center of the library
And he appears. Are we witnesses or actors?
The old man and the girl, smiling at one another,
He fixed by fame, she fluid, still without identity.
An instant which changes nothing,
And everything, forever, everything is changed.

from *The Paris Review*

PHYLLIS KOESTENBAUM

Admission of Failure

◊ ◊ ◊

The hostess seats a girl and a young man in a short-sleeve sport shirt with one arm missing below the shoulder. I'm at the next table with my husband and son, Andy's Barbecue Restaurant, an early evening in July, chewing a boneless rib eye, gulping a dark beer ordered from the cocktail waitress, a nervous woman almost over the hill, whose high heel sandals click back and forth from the bar to the dining room joined to the bar by an open arch. A tall heavy cook in white hat is brushing sauce on the chicken and spareribs rotating slowly on a squeaking spit. Baked potatoes heat on the oven floor. The young man is eating salad with his one hand. He and his girl are on a date. He has a forties' movie face, early Van Johnson before the motorcycle accident scarred his forehead. He lost the arm recently. Hard as it is, it could be worse. I would even exchange places with him if I could. *I want to exchange places with the young armless man in the barbecue restaurant.* He would sit at my table and I would sit at his. After dinner I would go in his car and he would go in mine. I would live in his house and work at his job and he would live in my house and do what I do. I would be him dressing and undressing and he would be me dressing and undressing. Our bill comes. My husband leaves the tip on the tray; we take toothpicks and mints and walk through the dark workingmen's bar out to the parking lot still lit by the sky though the streetlights have come on as they do automatically at the same time each night. We drive our son, home for the summer, back to his job at the bookstore. As old Italians and Jews say of sons from five to fifty, he's a good boy. I have worked on this paragraph for more than two years.

from *Epoch*

Mystery Stories

◇ ◇ ◇

THE TALKING CAT

I go to a performance. A man is talking about a woman and her cat. After the show, I meet the cat and he extends one of his front paws to shake my hand. He tells me he's happy to meet me and we have an instantaneous rapport. The woman seems jealous.

THE INDIAN

A regular guy turns into a tribal chief with gold and silver ornaments in his ears. He is also wearing bracelets and a beaded necklace. His father, the elder chief, comes in wearing a headdress and smiling.

POETRY

I give my poems to a man I have a crush on. He rolls them up and drops them into a plastic cup. He tells me he plans to read them later. I think they should be in a china cup.

THE RECORD STORE

A rock 'n' roller all dressed in black comes up behind me while I am flipping through albums in a record store. He kisses the top of my head. Later, he comes to visit a waiter at the restaurant where I am the manager or hostess.

The Red Coats

I wear two red coats to a party. I deposit them on the bed. When I go back to get them, one of them is gone. The one that is there is missing its top layer. It is not red anymore—it's grey with a black lining.

The Japanese Man

An old Japanese man is living alone on the outskirts of town. He feels sad and he is singing loudly about his bad fortune. I dream that I am this Japanese man. I wake up crying in the dream but not in real life.

Strawberries

I go to a restaurant that's like a nightclub in a 40's movie. At my table are three white plates filled with strawberries. No one else is there. I am afraid I will have to pay for their dinners when they come back.

from *Brooklyn Review*

Saga: Four Variations on the Sonnet

◇ ◇ ◇

1. LIFE STYLE

Invincible begetters, assorted Scutzes
have always lived hereabouts in the woods
trapping beaver or fox, poaching enough
deer to get by on. Winters, they barricade
their groundsills with spoiled hay, which can ignite
from a careless cigarette or chimney spark.
In the fifties, one family barely got out
when the place lit up like the Fair midway at dark.

The singular name of Scutz, it is thought, derives
from *skuft*, Middle Dutch for the nape one is strung up by.
Hangmen or hanged, they led the same snug lives
in an Old World loft adjoining the pigsty
as now, three generations tucked in two
rooms with color tv, in the New.

2. LEISURE

The seldom-traveled dirt road by their door
is where, good days, the Scutzes take their ease.
It serves as living room, garage, *pissoir*
as well as barnyard. Hens scratch and rabbits doze
under cars jacked up on stumps of trees.

Someone produces a dozen bottles of beer.
Someone tacks a target to a tire
across the road and hoists it seductively
human-high. The Scutzes love to shoot.
Later, they line the empty bottles up.

The music of glassbreak gladdens them. The brute
sound of a bullet widening a rip
in rubber, the rifle kick, the powder smell
pure bliss. Deadeyes, the Scutzes lightly kill.

3. SHELTER

Old doors slanted over packing crates
shelter the Scutzes' several frantic dogs
pinioned on six-foot chains they haven't been
loosed from since January of '91
when someone on skis crept up in snow fog
and undid all of their catches in the night.

Each of the Scutzes' dogs has a dish or plate
to eat from, usually overturned in the dirt.
What do they do for water? Pray for rain.
What do they do for warmth? Remember when
they lay in the litter together, a sweet
jumble of laundry, spotted and stained.

O we are smug in the face of the Scutzes, we
who stroll past their domain, its aromas of ripe decay,
its casual discards mottled with smut and pee.
What do we neighbors do? Look the other way.

4. SELF-FULFILLING PROPHECY

If Lonnie Scutz comes back, he's guaranteed
free room and board in the State's crowbar hotel.
His girlfriend Grace, a toddler at her heels
and in her arms a grubby ten-month jewel,
looks to be pregnant again, but not his seed.
It's rumored this one was sired by his dad.

Towheads with skyblue eyes, they'll go to school
now and then, struggle to learn to read
and write, forget to carry when they add,
be mocked, kept back or made to play the fool
and soon enough drop out. Their nimble code,
hit first or get hit, supplants the Golden Rule.

It all works out the way we knew it would.
They'll come to no good end, the Scutzes' kids.

from *Ploughshares*

Green

◇ ◇ ◇

and already the leaves have arrived,
my doctor, that blur of green you spoke of four years ago
thickened while you sat, spread in your chair in the sun,
children scuffing bicycles down the alley to the grocery store.
it was not really green, you said, but rather
a haze of green, a fog of green,
a thought of green you could only call light.

I awoke from a dream panicked
thinking I'd missed the arrival of the leaves.
a landlady was taking me from room to room,
each one barren and small and filled
with the sound of typewriters. there was a view
of a beach in the distance, the encroachment of a wave
like a finger, spray hitting the empty shore,
a foreign beach the color of dust.
the trees were black arms holding up the sky,
crookedly. along the sidewalk in front of the building
that fine mist, that vague rain of green had gone,
and the branches were bent with a new burden of leaves.

four years ago we had word-associated this thought of yours,
this green that wasn't there,
back when mysteries were still abundant
and could be uncovered. yesterday everything was plain

and unbudging as a jug sitting in the sun.
the beach was the color of your shirt, sand,
the color of your face new to the sun.

in the morning there was no way of telling
if the leaves had come, since there were only buildings,
every room a bleak room. the phone rang loudly
while you, my doctor, went hunting in the park for the hint
of green, the cloud of green you'd held in your mind
for four years, the green that was still mysterious
and therefore solvable, the green that failed to exist.
it breathed along the backs of your thick white hands
as the phone rang in my chest
without a sound, and you groped further and further
down the beach with the voice of the sands.

from *Michigan Quarterly Review*

This Hour and What Is Dead

◇ ◇ ◇

Tonight my brother, in heavy boots, is walking
through bare rooms over my head,
opening and closing doors.
What could he be looking for in an empty house?
What could he possibly need there in heaven?
Does he remember his earth, his birthplace set to torches?
His love for me feels like spilled water
running back to its vessel.

At this hour, what is dead is restless
and what is living is burning.

Someone tell him he should sleep now.

My father keeps a light on by our bed
and readies for our journey.
He mends ten holes at the knees
of five pairs of boys' pants.
His love for me is like his sewing:
too much thread and various colors,
the stitching uneven. But the needle pierces
clean through with each stroke of his hand.

At this hour, what is dead is worried
and what is living is fugitive.

Someone tell him he should sleep now.

God, that old furnace, keeps talking
with his mouth of teeth,
a beard stained at feasts, and his breath
of gasoline, airplane, human ash.
His love for me feels like fire,
feels like doves, feels like river water.

At this hour, what is dead is helpless, kind
and helpless. While the Lord lives.

Someone tell the Lord to leave me alone.
I've had enough of his love
that feels like burning and flight and running away.

from *Ploughshares*

DIONISIO D. MARTÍNEZ

Across These Landscapes of Early Darkness

◊ ◊ ◊

for Javier Menéndez López

He is learning to play the elegant songs
again. By ear. By heart. He is picking

up a signal from America, a faint humming,
a plea. He doesn't understand it. The elegant

music will suffice for the moment. This
time he will listen for the diesels slicing

the fog as they come up each morning,
their headlights leaving trails like a

photograph's version of life. There is elegance
in this, too. But there is more. A sense

of decorum as motif for a whole generation.
He is learning to live in style again. Here's

the suit for the nights when all
the stars are out and closer than usual

and some tradition says that you must count them.
Here's the pale shirt with no purpose.

Here are all the pointed shoes, all
the hats, the ties with the wrong patterns.

It is no one else's style. This makes it
more solid somehow, more durable. This

makes him happy. He hasn't laughed this
hard in years. He is picking up signals from

countries where the last transmission
took place light years ago. This is how

he learns about light years and how time
equals distance and distance is a kind

of salvation. He wants to come to America,
home of the faint signal, land of stolen

elegance. By now he has caught on
to the way we package someone else's tradition,

the way we price each package. These days
he is in the market for a new tradition.

It is all so obvious—the way we manufacture
our legacies. We are not the best of

thieves. Our music is always holding something
back, always looking for its source. He is

willing—at last—to take us as we are.
He runs to catch up, but by the time he manages

to get his hands on the essence of a song,
the song itself is light years from his hands.

from *Iowa Review*

All Hallows' Eve

◇ ◇ ◇

A mouse
gnaws a hole
in the white grain sack of sky.
Night spills everywhere.

Small ghost
racing for a hiding place

but only fields loom up
wide and starless and low.

Knotted tight
at wrist and neck—
the dirty bed sheet

she will have to live in
for as long as red leaves fall.

And what costume
is *he* wearing this time—
Raphael, Lucifer,

father? Tall as the balding
moon, he splits
a doll's face

as he steps near enough
for the flames
stitched into sour wings

to scissor
their golden tips deep
into his daughter's
lamé skin.

from *North American Review*

JAMES McCORKLE

". . . The Storm is Passing Over"; She Sang

◇ ◇ ◇

Windows collect the late effulgence, as though wings
Ripped from angels were hung on racks
Draped with pearls, the frames fired by cinnabar.
Above us, the spheres have been plotted
And set as silent architectures without the cracks
That mark settling and routine when life is ajar
But sound, the angles held in place, singing.

The clouds to the south engorged with snow,
Push toward us, while scavengers poke black trash bags
And plastic sheets tacked over windows ripple.
The air heaves with light, the tempest like Giorgione's—
Though his belongs to another season: trees spring from crags
Of the city a soft verdure has scaled, where we are coupled
With a youth and a mother in deepened time over the river's bar.

Neither greet us, though one looks steadily past us,
Toward a final point or the one that commences the lines
Of sight that radiate, touching building, bridge, storm.
What she must watch is our slow dismantling
Of the scene—the still trees or storm are signs
For what is coming, behind our backs, no alarm
Given but a stretch of silence like a widening timbal.

A pack of white and gray flecked grackles scour
Vines of their dried berries, the brightness
Now belongs to the snow, covering everything—nothing left.
In the distance derricks lift huge containers into holds
Of ships, gulls swept with the snow's relentlessness
Are drawn up, past the sheetmetal sky, following the theft
Of arras stitched with an angel's fiery arm.

Who could draw us away from that scene,
The space a reliquary for past and future,
The light diving to the inner corners of rooms.
The clouds split open over Giorgione's city, no one crosses
The bridge that rises in place of the horizon's tenure—
Nearby everything shimmers, the page you hold is a loom
Shuttling over vacancy—the river's or sky's cleft.

And what has touched us in the past
Still unfurls around us, signals something, a flare
Arcing over the buildings toward the sea.
And what offerings could we make with an epoch at its close,
Except follow the disappearing lines in the snow-pocked air,
Fiery embers dropping, each a key
To the insweeping darkness the snow festoons.

from *Verse*

Terminal

◊   ◊   ◊

All the significant lines, above and below, intersect at the border.
The guards of the border guard these lines.
We all ride those lines, back and forth, every day.
The border is where one's ride stops, where you get out.

The merry-go-rounds are for children only, or for adults
who choose to go in circles. Likewise the slides,
for whom the corresponding image is a rapid, smooth decline.
The Tunnel is for lovers who choose not to see each other.

The machines of the border enumerate and mark.
Your number is "1"; your mark means nothing.
The border's chief virtue is efficiency, every line
numbered, marked, and made to run on time.

House of Science, House of Art, House of Money, House of War:
these are the barracks of the guards of the border.
Beyond the border, they say, you do not wish to pass.
They say beyond the border lie more, more terrible borders.

from *Callaloo*

Choosing an Author for Assurance in the Night

◇　◇　◇

I hoped it would be someone
who, burning through her last mask,
debuting with the creases earned
    from its petrified pillow,
      would show me how
      to live persistently.
Reject (I asked) the hollow protection
    of your headdress,
      mystagogue, inspirator,
         its copper
    wires and antelope skin,
its bronze or cam wood or coconut hair.

    But I had to turn
to the lean idol of this Day of the Dead
compulsive writer in her afterlife,
    whose own fine fittings have slipped.
      She's hung them up with her fencing mesh
      and catcher's grille.
She types:
    "I know now
      to be plain, with an occasional seed
        leafing out from my sutures.
    I am bony as a bridge,
a bare letter-by-letter pusher,

assembled in angles
to span.
Death makes me direct,
    with a little ornamental nonsense
      of elbows and knees,
      if you call this death:
my twaddle still counsels
      though I have no ears to hook a mask on.
        'Carver, coppersmith, make me a disguise,'
        you won't hear me saying.
    My typing fingers fly
up to my face

    like a plunging pianist's.
Accurate, flexible, but not bravura.
So for the sacred ritual
    around the fire
      I will not be chosen;
      to chant
one needs the scored shell of an artist,
    the scarifications
      of a decorator to look out through,
        pod eyes, tube eyes,
    to breathe through, to
tug an audience through with

    innuendo, wooden winks.
Now, I like my skull
but it won't get me the priestesshood.
    I like my skull;
      it got me here."
                And here—
    close beside me.
The blood is running around in my hand
    to keep up with her messages
    from,

it feels like,
one of those colossal stones
that throw starlight.

from *Field*

Honey

◇   ◇   ◇

Only calmness will reassure
the bees to let you rob their hoard.
Any sweat of fear provokes them.
Approach with confidence, and from
the side, not shading their entrance.
And hush smoke gently from the spout
of the pot of rags, for sparks will
anger them. If you go near bees
every day they will know you.
And never jerk or turn so quick
you excite them. If weeds are trimmed
around the hive they have access
and feel free. When they taste your smoke
they fill themselves with honey and
are laden and lazy as you
lift the lid to let in daylight.
No bee full of sweetness wants to
sting. Resist greed. With the top off
you touch the fat gold frames, each cell
a hex perfect as a snowflake,
a sealed relic of sun and time
and roots of many acres fixed
in crystal-tight arrays, in rows
and lattices of sweeter latin
from scattered prose of meadow, woods.

from *The Atlantic Monthly*

THYLIAS MOSS

An Anointing

◇ ◇ ◇

Boys have to slash their fingers to become brothers. Girls
trade their Kotex, me and Molly do in the mall's public facility.

Me and Molly never remember each other's birthdays. On purpose.
We don't like scores of any kind. We don't wear watches or weigh
ourselves.

Me and Molly have tasted beer. We drank our shampoo. We went
to the doctor together and lifted our specimen cups in a toast. We
didn't drink that stuff. We just gargled.

When me and Molly get the urge, we are careful to put it back
exactly as we found it. It looks untouched.

Between the two of us, me and Molly have 20/20 vision.

Me and Molly are in eighth grade for good. We like it there.
We adore the view. We looked both ways and decided not to cross the
street. Others who'd been to the other side didn't return. It was
a trap.

Me and Molly don't double date. We don't multiply anything. We
don't know our multiplication tables from a coffee table. We'll never
be decent waitresses, indecent ones maybe.

Me and Molly do not believe in going ape or going bananas or going
Dutch. We go as who we are. We go as what we are.

Me and Molly have wiped each other's asses with ferns. Made emergency tampons of our fingers. Me and Molly make do with what we have.

Me and Molly are in love with wiping the blackboard with each other's hair. The chalk gives me and Molly an idea of what old age is like; it is dusty and makes us sneeze. We are allergic to it.

Me and Molly, that's M and M, melt in your mouth.

What are we doing in your mouth? Me and Molly bet you'll never guess. Not in a million years. We plan to be around that long. Together that long. Even if we must freeze the moment and treat the photograph like the real thing.

Me and Molly don't care what people think. We're just glad that they do.

Me and Molly lick the dew off the morning grasses but taste no honey till we lick each other's tongues.

We wear full maternity sails. We boat upon my broken water. The katabatic action begins, Molly down my canal binnacle first, her water breaking in me like an anointing.

from *Epoch*

CAROL MUSKE

Red Trousseau

◊　◊　◊

"What is woman but a foe to friendship . . ."
MALLEUS MALEFICARUM
(*Witches' Hammer,* 1494)

I.

Because she desired him,
and feared desire, the room
readied itself for judgment:
though they were nothing to
each other, maybe friends,
maybe a man and a woman
seated at a table
　　　　beneath a skylight
through which light poured,
interrogatory.

II.

Because his face always appears to her
half in shadow,
　　　　she chooses finally
to distrust him and her seared memory,

even though it was noon, when the sun
hovers in its guise of impatient tribunal,
seizing every contradiction in dismissive brilliance:

the white cloth, their separate folded hands,
a mock-crucible holding fire-veined blossoms.
No, it was a bowl of fruit, a glass of red wine,
the simplest, thoughtless vessel, that was it,
wasn't it, held up, like this, an offering?

III.

Reading the accounts of the trials,
late at night, she sees that the questions
must have begun in a friendly, almost desultory
fashion: rising slowly in pitch and intensity,
to reveal, finally, God's bright murderous gaze,
the mouth of the trap. Conviction required stigmata,
the search for the marks of Hell's love on the un-male
body, the repetitive testimony of men: that she midwifed
the stillborn, curdled milk, spied, screamed at climax,
grew wings—and worse, *Looking over her shoulder,*
I saw her laughing he said *laughing at me*

till, at the end, days later, she could feel
her way eagerly, blind, cleansed of memory,
through the maze of metal doors to the last door:
the single depthless mirror.

IV.

They were already disappearing, sitting there together
talking in a forthright way, laughing, unaware of their
faces reflected, enlarged like cult images, effigies:
dark hair, light hair. Already the ancient lens
sliding into place between them, whose purpose is not
to clarify sight, but rather to magnify, magnify till
its capacity for difference ignites.

Tell me why it was only his gaze on her,
why his right to primary regard, *her* life under scrutiny,
her life reduced to some fatal lack of irony, naïve midwife
to this monstrous *please*?
                    See how the lens bends the light
into what amounts now to tinder . . .
                    So sight can come, now, heatedly
alive, living wood, corrected

V.

I admit now that I never felt sympathy for her,
as she stood there burning in the abstract.
Though condemned by her own body
(the ridiculous tonsured hair, bare feet
and bruised cheek, as if she'd been pushed up
against a headboard in passionate love)—
I suspected her mind of collaboration,
apperceptive ecstasy, the flames wrapped
about her like a red trousseau, yes,
the dream of immolation.

But look at the way her lips move—
it is the final enlightenment. Below
the nailed sign of her craft
                    are the words published
from her lover's mouth
the mouth of the friend who betrayed her:
her naked body, his head on her breast
like a child's *heal me*—
and her answer?

God, tell me there was a moment
when she could have willed herself into language,
just once, into her own stammering, radical defense:

I am worth saving

before the flames breathed imperious at her feet
before her mouth, bewitched, would admit to anything

from *American Poetry Review*

Rain

◇   ◇   ◇

1.

All afternoon it rained, then
such power came down from the clouds
on a yellow thread,
as authoritative as God is supposed to be.
When it hit the tree, her body
opened forever.

2. THE SWAMP

Last night, in the rain, some of the men climbed over
   the barbed-wire fence of the detention center.
In the darkness they wondered if they could do it, and knew
   they had to try to do it.
In the darkness they climbed the wire, handful after handful
   of barbed wire.
Even in the darkness most of them were caught and sent back
   to the camp inside.
But a few are still climbing the barbed wire, or wading through
   the blue swamp on the other side.

What does barbed wire feel like when you grip it, as though
   it were a loaf of bread, or a pair of shoes?
What does barbed wire feel like when you grip it, as though
   it were a plate and a fork, or a handful of flowers?

What does barbed wire feel like when you grip it, as though
    it were the handle of a door, working papers, a clean sheet
    you want to draw over your body?

3.

Or this one: on a rainy day, my uncle
lying in the flower bed,
cold and broken,
dragged from the idling car
with its plug of rags, and its gleaming
length of hose. My father
shouted,
then the ambulance came,
then we all looked at death,
then the ambulance took him away.
From the porch of the house
I turned back once again
looking for my father, who had lingered,
who was still standing in the flowers,
who was that motionless muddy man,
who was that tiny figure in the rain.

4. EARLY MORNING, MY BIRTHDAY

The snails on the pink sleds of their bodies are moving
    among the morning glories.
The spider is asleep among the red thumbs
    of the raspberries.
What shall I do, what shall I do?

The rain is slow.
The little birds are alive in it.
Even the beetles.
The green leaves lap it up.
What shall I do, what shall I do?

The wasp sits on the porch of her paper cast
The blue heron floats out of the clouds.
The fish leap, all rainbow and mouth, from the dark water.

This morning the water lilies are no less lovely, I think,
     than the lilies of Monet.
And I do not want anymore to be useful, to be docile, to lead
children out of the fields into the text
of civility, to teach them that they are (they are not) better
     than the grass.

5. At the Edge of the Ocean

I have heard this music before,
saith the body.

6. The Garden

The kale's
puckered sleeve,
the pepper's
hollow bell,
the lacquered onion.

Beets, borage, tomatoes.
Green beans.

I came in and I put everything
on the counter: chives, parsley, dill,
the squash like a pale moon,
peas in their silky shoes, the dazzling
rain-drenched corn.

7. THE FOREST

At night
under the trees
the black snake
jellies forward
rubbing
roughly
the stems of the bloodroot,
the yellow leaves,
little boulders of bark,
to take off
the old life.
I don't know
if he knows
what is happening.
I don't know
if he knows
it will work.
In the distance
the moon and the stars
give a little light.
In the distance
the owl cries out.

In the distance
the owl cries out.
The snake knows
these are the owl's woods,
these are the woods of death,

these are the woods of hardship
where you crawl and crawl,
where you live in the husks of trees,
where you lie on the wild twigs
and they cannot bear your weight,
where life has no purpose
and is neither civil nor intelligent.

Where life has no purpose,
and is neither civil nor intelligent,
it begins
to rain,
it begins
to smell like the bodies
of flowers.
At the back of the neck
the old skin splits.
The snake shivers
but does not hesitate.
He inches forward.
He begins to bleed through
like satin.

from Poetry

Eighth Sky

◊ ◊ ◊

It is scribbled along the body
Impossible even to say a word

An alphabet has been stored beneath the ground
It is a practice alphabet, work of the hand

Yet not, not marks inside a box
For example, this is a mirror box

Spinoza designed such a box
and called it the Eighth Sky

called it the Nevercadabra House
as a joke

Yet not, not so much a joke
not Notes for Electronic Harp

on a day free of sounds
(but I meant to write "clouds")

At night these same boulevards fill with snow
Lancers and dancers pass a poisoned syringe,

as you wrote, writing of death in the snow,
Patroclus and a Pharaoh on Rue Ravignan

It is scribbled across each body
Impossible even to name a word

Look, you would say, how the sky falls
at first gently, then not at all

Two chemicals within the firefly are the cause
Twin ships, twin nemeses

preparing to metamorphose
into an alphabet in stone

St.-Benoît-sur-Loire
to Max Jacob

from *Grand Street*

Avenue

◇ ◇ ◇

They stack bright pyramids of goods and gather
Mop-helves in sidewalk barrels. They keen, they boogie.
Paints, fruits, clean bolts of cottons and synthetics,
Clarity and plumage of October skies.

Way of the costermonger's wooden barrow
And also the secular marble cinquefoil and lancet
Of the great store. They persist. The jobber tells
The teller in the bank and she retells

Whatever it is to the shopper and the shopper
Mentions it to the retailer by the way.
They mutter and stumble, derelict. They write
These theys I write. Scant storefront pushbroom Jesus

Of Haitian hardware—they travel in shadows, they flog
Sephardic softgoods. They strain. Mid-hustle they faint
And shrivel. Or snoring on grates they rise to thrive.
Bonemen and pumpkins of All Saints. Kol Nidre,

Blunt shovel of atonement, a blade of song
From terra cotta temple: Lord, forgive us
Our promises, we chant. Or we churn our wino
Syllables and stares on the Avenue. We, they—

Jack. Mrs. Whisenant from the bakery. Sam Lee.
This is the way, its pavement crackwork burnished
With plantain. In strollers they bawl and claw. They flourish.
Furniture, Florist, Pets. My mongrel tongue

Of *nudnik* and *criminentlies*, the tarnished flute
And brogue of quidnuncs in the bars, in Casey's
Black amber air of spent Hiram Walker, attuned.
Sweet ash of White Owl. Ten High. They touch. Eyes blurred

Stricken with passion as in a Persian lyric
They flower and stroke. They couple. From the Korean,
Staples and greens. From the Christian Lebanese,
Home electronics. Why is that Friday "Good"?

Why "Day of Atonement" for release from vows?
Because we tried us, to be at one, because
We say as one we traffic, we dice, we stare.
Some they remember that won't remember them—

Their headlights found me stoned, like a bundled sack
Lying in the Avenue, late. They didn't speak
My language. For them, a small adventure. They hefted
Me over the curb and bore me to an entry

Out of the way. Illuminated footwear
On both sides. How I stank. Dead drunk. They left me
Breathing in my bower between the Halloween
Brogans and pumps on crystal pedestals.

But I was dead to the world. The midnight city
In autumn. Day of attainment, tall saints
Who saved me. My taints, day of anointment. Oil
Of rose and almond in the haircutting parlor,

Motor oil swirling rainbows in gutter water.
Ritually unattainted, the congregation
File from the place of worship and resume
The rumbling drum and hautbois of conversation,

Speech of the granary, of the cloven lanes
Of traffic, of salvaged silver. Not shriven and yet
Not rent, they stride the Avenue, banter, barter.
Capering, on fire, they cleave to the riven hub.

from *The Boston Phoenix*

LAWRENCE RAAB

The Sudden Appearance
of a Monster at a Window

◇ ◇ ◇

Yes, his face really is so terrible
you cannot turn away. And only
that thin sheet of glass between you,
clouding with his breath.
Behind him: the dark scribbles of trees
in the orchard, where you walked alone
just an hour ago, after the storm had passed,
watching water drip from the gnarled branches,
stepping carefully over the sodden fruit.
At any moment he could put his fist
right through that window. And on your side:
you could grab hold of something like
this letter opener, or even now you could try
very slowly to slide the revolver
out of the drawer in the desk
where you're sitting, where you were writing
a letter which is there in front of you.
But none of this will happen. And not because
you feel sorry for him, or detect
in his scarred face some helplessness
that shows in your own as compassion.
You will never know what he wanted,
what he might have done, since
this thing, of its own accord, turns away.
And because yours is a life in which

such a monster cannot figure for long,
you compose yourself, and return
to your letter about the storm, how it bent
the apple trees so low they dragged
on the ground, ruining the harvest.

from *Denver Quarterly*

LIAM RECTOR

The Night the Lightning Bugs Lit Last in the Field Then Went Their Way

◇　◇　◇

We went out into the field to get away from the others, to make
love, and there they were—hundreds of them—lighting their last night
in the shudder, the quickening cold, the shifting weather come then

to gather them in . . . Towards what? Anything there for us, after?
Already hundreds had gone down but surely this was the last evening
even for the strongest among them, and as the cold entered us we went

quickly down. . . . First you on top of me, then with your legs
　　　wrapped
around me and me pushing as deeply as I could, going into you, as if
there were some great depth I would not be having the time to go into.

from *Agni Review*

Plenitude

◇　◇　◇

Ignore them. They are only beautiful
and heartless—not because of the unmoving
seascape behind them, the august rays crowning
pacific, glassy water in leviathan's
heavenly backdrop, but because they mean
to tell us that our freedom is a machine.
It is not. It cannot be redesigned
nor can it carry us to a new place.
We are here, where history placed us,
history that always waited modestly
for our consent, sure of receiving it.
Those beautiful young people standing
beside the automobile in the surf
agreed to nothing. If there is such a thing
as a new place, it belongs to them,
and the water will be heaven there and life
pacific in the rosy stare of the ideal.
Ignore them. Let us love our lives. No one
ever truly fled from a suburb.
He was expelled or shamed or too easily
angered. And when he left, his heart broke.
He fell easy prey to the beautiful
and to the falsehoods of seascape and landscape
with no one moving upon them as leviathan's
obsessed challenger. Our houses are buoys
set upon restless waters by strangers
dead when we were born. But we live

inside them now, and freedom is no machine
to motor us in empty circles and to raise
a round wake behind us. Freedom is a dwelling.
Sometimes, in the small arcades of a watercolor
bought at the yard sales, brass-lighted in a corner
by a chair, you have helped yourself to a dream
that drowned whalers, kin of yours, return from sea.
A holiday mood and others, like yourself,
living nearby, hurry in from the night's damp
and talk the small talk with no thought for sleeping.
Then at morning, suddenly through the west window,
birds flare golden with flying into sunrise.
It feels like driving sometimes, but the music
is not tinny and the light is slow,
bell-towered from east to west with the morning.
Annisquam. Swampscott. Marblehead. Scituate.
Do not ignore these. Inconstant, mawkish but
deep in the old physical sense of depth,
the voluntary hours with neighbors and ghosts
teach the beauty of commuting
from dark to light, from labor to home life:
a vigilance crowned with impatience and visited
rarely but adequately by golden changes.

2.

Appreciation is mania.
Neighbors can be too many neighbors,
and cold, upturned shoals of seaboard towns
too many churches, too many conversions.

I know the stained glass above a doorway
is the discomfited piety of change
and light destroying what it makes only
to remake it more beautifully.
Such things make one thing clear: as betrayer
speaks to innocent, liar speaks to liar.

A vigil crowned with gentians
survives as disappointed love.
Visitations of impatience
take away our hands and home life.

Treason we learn from the childless small talk
of nights whose sheltering adjustments gall us.
When I first betrayed someone
an angel fell backwards through the air's sheen.
When I next betrayed someone
the air lost its heart, which is love's density.

I was at seaside in an old town,
and sea and housefronts brightened but did not open.
I was upon the point of prayer when the light
froze, converted from churchlight to porchlight.

We betray our homes because they are valuable.
No reason not to make the fine distinctions still:
we live only half-expecting the sudden flares,
or affection, or seasons out of the sea weather,
as expectations and good friends shelter by us
from the darkness of streets we've blackened together.

Five o'clock in the morning
is not four o'clock in the morning.
I have betrayed each and might betray
all in the spotless, glassy piety of change.

3.

But how hotly change limits
happiness: the small happiness of possession
and the even smaller of self-possession.
Imagine yourself transient among these houses
and the uncontrolled reflection of hotel hours
when no one in the hallway or next room

depends on you. Already darkness covers
the tilted Common outside your window.
You hear a school band playing carols.
As always and everywhere, there are too many
drums. An hour earlier, in twilight,
you were out walking, looking into the shops,
handling the used books and scented soaps,
humming a little distracted by a late lunch
and the brown New England drinks hotly perfect
at Christmas. So many minutiae, so many parts
played by drums against the unsteady, truer
lines of the horns. In angular twilight,
unfocussed and sullen clusters of teen-agers,
underdressed and loudly self-aware,
anticipating nothing of change, feeling none
of the desolate childlessness of Christmas,
jostled you, marred the picturesque of the darkening
Common, and drove you back indoors.
Those same teen-agers are perfectly
reconfigured in the night now, playing
carols or holding candles as the merchants' trees
come to light. The shoppers join in then
and lift their children up to see what you
see from a hotel window: something
perfect, an incidental miracle
taking no notice of a transient
or his cold need to interpret convincingly
accidents in the lightsome context of personal
history or a fictive changelessness.
You could be a returning mariner
stealing a welcome properly due to those
who cannot return. You feel childless
but as though a child is coming, perhaps
from among those children out there
trumpeting mock-starlight, or from
farther away, from the black ocean beyond
the Common. Where will you not be barren?
Where will you not prayerfully resist change

to the death or to the last drum-tap
of the disorganized religion of sorrow?
Sometimes, however lonely, a wealth beyond your reach
is enough wealth, the plenitude of the lives
of strangers is enough life, enough to prove
the world adequate to desire though still strange.

4.

And when I have enough, am I afraid
no longer? When desire flutters its last
broken wheel in the red west and day
falls into the arms of wife and of child's laughter,

is it satiety or just the beginning
of fear's moment, the early dismantling
and inland birds suddenly trapped
in coastal cry, in the gulls they are not,
or is it really annihilation wrapped
in a premonition I had almost forgotten?

Between history, that topography of roofs,
and freedom, that indirect solitude
housing neither a first marriage nor echo
of a newborn's dream cries, runs a fly-blown

cheerless corridor of air.
It is the windy premonition of nothing
to desire. It lauds the greater pleasures
of the immediate present where all things
depend on paraphrase and the betrayal
of history to fiction, of freedom to delay.

Between transience, that Christmas hostelry,
and home, where I once found time to make
fine distinctions capable of taking
words or a tiny hand and of seeing

the democracy in it, the warm sufficiency,
runs a mania of years like adulteries.
Those years are full. They transform tirelessly
inland creatures to sea-birds, inland towns
to capes and to submissive widows
of coastline where strangers assume the dead's renown.

Though ever strange, though nearly adequate,
the world's, or to speak honestly, my life's
suburban intervals lose buoyancy like
birds unused to tides or to wracks of net.

5.

In sinking or in being caught in nets
we find a lonely, accidental escape,
something to do with music on the radio
of an automobile, the tinny, driving, middle
distances of houses and neighborhoods
like the buoys of strangers calling us back
to life though not to our own lives, opening
as the undertow opens on the first evening
of a full moon, as sky does on the mornings
when sunrise and moonset are one hour.
I am sure that something happens.
The world is too full not to rescue
what loses buoyancy or becomes trapped.
The fullness makes a protest, and its proposal
is labor, that needle-sharp history
that follows everyone to his remote place
and serves him there. And if we refuse rescue,
we do so because we cannot believe
that fullness and innocence (a child coming also
from near the ocean) inhabit the same places,
haunt the same sidestreets and rock formations
in amateur choirs, in the brass-lit, private hum
of landscapes carefully miniaturized

by our pleasure in fullness and selfless love
for the innocent cradled in futurity
or the miraculous. These are accidental colleagues
forever bound to one another, often in love.
I got up early and went out walking
deep into woods that betrayed nothing
of ocean except the wound it makes on air.
I came to a compound barrier of rocks
beyond which I saw nothing and above which
the air was crystals of jagged salt turning
to murk. Like an exhalation, spume appeared
and then black water edging under the spray
toward me in tendrils. There was a water rat
soaked and trembling on the barrier,
coruscated, unsure of what to fear:
the advancing tide and tendriled backwash
or me, hooded in a raincoat, standing between him
and dry land, his only future and safety.
There is no difference worth noting
between thinking of oneself as "you" or "I,"
between the impostor and the true mariner.
Better to ignore the difference and believe
that the unseen ocean is no machine
but the irrepressible origin of many freedoms,
many dwellings. I stepped back into the woods,
and the rat dashed past me into common futures
of small arcades and enough welcome.

from *New Letters*

For a Friend in Travail

◇   ◇   ◇

Waking from violence: the surgeon's probe left in the foot
paralyzing the body from the waist down.
Dark before dawn: wrapped in a shawl, to walk the house
the Drinking-Gourd slung in the northwest,
half-slice of moon to the south
through dark panes.   A time to speak to you.

What are you going through? she said, is the great question.
Philosopher of oppression, theorist
of the victories of force.

We write from the marrow of our bones.   What she did not
ask, or tell: how victims save their own lives.

That crawl along the ledge, then the ravelling span of fibre
                    strung
from one side to the other, I've dreamed that too.
Waking, not sure we made it.   Relief, appallment, of waking.
Consciousness.   O, no.   To sleep again.
O to sleep without dreaming.

How day breaks, when it breaks, how clear and light the moon
melting into moon-colored air
moist and sweet, here on the western edge.

Love for the world, and we are part of it.
How the poppies break from their sealed envelopes
she did not tell.

What are you going through, there on the other edge?

from *Poetry*

We Sat, So Patient

◇ ◇ ◇

We sat, so patient, in that third
   grade
class, learning the numbers of days,
   weeks, months,
repeating the numbers as they flashed
   in the air, forming
the curved 3, the angular 4, the easy 1,
adding them up, subtracting, multiplying
   and dividing
as though we owned them, and we did,
   then,
counting the rain drops that wriggled down
   the gray window,
counting the hearts and cars on our desks,
   our crayons,
Ann Harden and Richie Freeman making 2,
10 on each side for the spelling bee,
   counting silent
seconds when Sister Ann Zita said 5
   of us
would not reach 20, showed the chart
where children dropped off into 0,
   the blue zone of No Return
that Jimmy Legasse whispered, making us laugh.
Looking around, I thought Al Aubon, Jackie Foster,
   Dorothy Blake

who already coughed blood on her gold glasses
  when she spoke,
the thin girl just come over from Germany,
and Ray Martineau who had no lunch, the
  zigzagged
white lines of lice forming mazes on his
  crewcut head. And
the good Sister herself, number 6, at least
  40 years older than us,
her rosary beads clicking as she walked
down the aisle like the Angel of Death,
  black
wings spread, brushing our faces, our arms,
  wafting blackness
into our eyes, our lungs, our hearts,
reminding us that God was watching and could tell
  who knew 9 times 9, 144 divided by 12,
telling us it was God's will that we die,
Jimmy Gleason pulling up his white sock
on a leg he would not have 10 years later,
Barbara Ryan raising her hand with another
  correct answer,
the same hand so whitish-blue as she lay
  in her eighth-grade coffin,
Jimmy Amyot and Donald Wilcox quietly passing
  drawings of naked women
back and forth, the car they would die in
  revving
unheard in that classroom where we yelled
  out 360, 225, 32, 0, 10,
waiting for the split-second flash of red,
  yellow and blue cards
beneath the slow, steadily clicking clock.

from *Boulevard*

DAVID ST. JOHN

Lucifer in Starlight

◇ ◇ ◇

"Tired of his dark dominion . . ."
—GEORGE MEREDITH

It was something I'd overheard
One evening at a party; a man I liked enormously
          Saying to a mutual friend, a woman
Wearing a vest embroidered with scarlet and violet tulips
     That belled below each breast, "Well, I've always
Preferred Athens; Greece seems to me a country
          Of the day—Rome, I'm afraid, strikes me
As being a city of the night . . ."
          Of course, I knew instantly just what he meant—
          Not simply because I love
Standing on the terrace of my apartment on a clear evening
     As the constellations pulse low in the Roman sky,
The whole mind of night that I know so well
          Shimmering in its elaborate webs of infinite,
Almost divine irony. No, and it wasn't only that Rome
     Was *my* city of the night, that it was here I'd chosen
          To live when I grew tired of my ancient life
As the Underground Man. And it wasn't that Rome's darkness
          Was of the kind that consoles so many
     Vacancies of the soul; my Rome, with its endless history
Of falls . . . No, it was that this dark was the deep, sensual dark
     Of the dreamer; this dark was like the violet fur
Spread to reveal the illuminated nipples of
          The She-Wolf—all the sequins above in sequence,

The white buds lost in those fields of ever-deeping gentians,
    A dark like the polished back of a mirror,
        The pool of the night scalloped and hanging
Above me, the inverted reflection of a last,
                Odd Narcissus . . .

           One night my friend Nico came by
Close to three A.M.—As we drank a little wine, I could see
        The black of her pupils blown wide,
The spread ripples of the opiate night . . . And Nico
      Pulled herself close to me, her mouth almost
         Touching my mouth, as she sighed, "Look . . . ,"
And deep within the pupil of her left eye,
      Almost like the mirage of a ship's distant, hanging
      Lantern rocking with the waves,
I could see, at the most remote end of the receding,
    Circular hallway of her eye, there, at its doorway,
At the small aperture of the black telescope of the pupil,
        A tiny, dangling crucifix—
Silver, lit by the ragged shards of starlight, reflecting
    In her as quietly as pain, as simply as pain . . .
Some years later, I saw Nico on stage in New York, singing
    Inside loosed sheets of shattered light, a fluid
Kaleidoscope washing over her—the way any naked,
        Emerging Venus steps up along the scalloped lip
Of her shell, innocent and raw as fate, slowly
Obscured by a fluorescence that reveals her simple, deadly
        Love of sexual sincerity . . .
    I didn't bother to say hello. I decided to remember
The way in Rome, out driving at night, she'd laugh as she let
    Her head fall back against the cracked, red leather
        Of my old Lancia's seats, the soft black wind
Fanning her pale, chalky hair out along its currents,
    Ivory waves of starlight breaking above us in the leaves;
The sad, lucent malevolence of the heavens, falling . . .

Both of us racing silently as light. Nowhere,
Then forever . . .
Into the mind of the Roman night.

from *Denver Quarterly*

Trial

◊　◊　◊

When I worked at the Denny's in downtown Milwaukee—mostly at
　the counter,
never advancing, except for someone's break, to a section with
　booths—
one of the cooks I worked with was this really short guy, five feet,
　maybe, and ugly.
who, rumor had it, was back from Vietnam and out on parole for one
　of the violent fits he'd had.
You could tell at work, he was hanging onto that routine:

everything, every piece of bacon, every garnish was meticulously laid,
and because he'd get mad if it seemed you didn't care, and slow your
　order down,
I took to flirting with him and, during the afternoon breaks we had,
listening to the wartime stories he'd tell. I hated hearing them
and the way he turned the kerchief around his neck: it was like he was
　twisting

his confession out and, afterward, too, the way he looked at me,
like I really had it, the power to hand him his pardon.
The closest to grace he probably ever got was oblivion, getting blasted
every night after work on booze and grass mostly, but once I sold him
　some acid,
this great blue-tab stuff my boyfriend, who'd gone back to New York,
　had given me.

It was a while before we worked it out: $5 a tab, $12 for the three.
He said he was going to drop—finally bomb the gooks out—
in the middle of the Kettle Moraine, a wilderness of rolling hills
and horse trails where there's little, if anything, to be ambushed by,
but I don't know if that's where he really went, or if he'd ever
    dropped before:

maybe he freaked out at the bar he usually haunted, not just hurting
    himself,
but dragging along one of the guys who kept his vigils with him,
or, at home, it was his wife he went for, or his kids for all I know,
but whatever it was, it was heavy enough for the narcs to show up at
    work questioning everyone.
I was in the basement, just coming out of the change room before my
    shift,

and I remember looking down at my very white shoes—there was a
    fine for the unpolished—
my name tag, my brown skirt, and orange apron. There I was in that
    uniform
facing what looked like the dark-suited agents from one of Kafka's
    hells,
and it hit me then that there was real trouble here, but I could see,
    too,
from the routine way they prodded, that it was nothing I'd ever have
    to enter,

nothing anyone would ever pin on me and that, already, we'd left him,
some twisted guy at the end of a small and worthless transaction.

from *Western Humanities Review*

Good Friday. Driving Westward.

◇ ◇ ◇

. . . being by others hurried every day,
Scarce in a yeare their naturall forme obey:
Pleasure or businesse, so our Soules admit
For their first mover, and are whirld by it.
                                    —JOHN DONNE

The rain. Rain that will not end.
The daily errands. Daily bread.
No letting up. No pause
as I steer blindly, circling
the great city. City of tears and blood.
I woke this morning to the ringing phone.
To the last days of the twentieth century.
Hello. Hello. But the line was dead.
The phone in my hand heavy.
My mind whirling. Numb. Taken
against my will closer to oblivion.
At the mall, a man in rags begging
for a coin. My God, only a coin!
I turned my back. Turned back.
But he was gone. Daily, I turn my back.
The suffering of others more and more
like television. Do I drive East? West?
Do I suffer? Shall anger be divine?
Uncorrected, I steer. Swerve

on a slick patch. Lose control.
The rain letting up now. Clouds torn.
The setting sun a brilliant bloody globe.
As if a nailed hand had violently
raked the sky. And then withdrawn.
Past anger or mercy. Leaving me
more distanced. Alone. Driving
this endless road with all the others.
Night and night's Eternity coming on.

from *The New Criterion*

I Want to Marry You

◇　◇　◇

I want to marry you,
I want to fingerfuck a gold hole.
I'm a fossil, perfectly preserved.
You could excavate me from the cold guts
of this tough jewel, could chip away
chunks and brush sharp dust
from my lips as I whispered, take me wholly,
make me whole.
Take me up to a high hot town.
In a room done in dry rough gold cleaned clean
I will gingerly rest my ass, test the bed for groans and gives.
You'll bring me fishy water in a glass.
I will drink it, I will lie
in foreign darkness, watch my feet
reach above the blue moving desert of your back
for the moon, from which I'll try
to wring a little honey.
Honey, sun will ring off rocks,
will sting us for a week or two.
Our life will be a slap, a sneeze.
Oh, how I'll wish you would put down
that magazine and look the hell at me.
But I will never take my dress off.
I will never take my dress off, the white one,
the right one, the holey lacy binding binding
tight one.
I will swim in stone again,

wearing my dress. I will emerge,
wetter than ever, wearing my best dress.
But your face will remain buried in the gloss
of pages, and I will bury myself
in fishy pool water
til I'm dredged from the depth of that juicy jewel
by another man who will not have managed
to save my life.
Stiff and dripping, dressed in white,
I will embrace the cooking, empty air.
In a new voice thick with love, you'll say,
hey, mister, that's my wife you've got there.
But he will not hear you, he will be dancing
for me, for me. He'll dance a wild
shapeless dance, his unclean fist
bashing the skin of a shimmering tambourine,
his icy taps chiseling a random rhythm in the rock
for me. And honey,
his chaotic music will riddle me til
I'm half again the girl I used to be, til
I'm senseless, perforated ecstasy,
til I'm holy.

from *Another Chicago Magazine*

Anatolian Journey

◊   ◊   ◊

Impedimenta of the self
Left behind somewhere, or traded
For a bag with good straps, a book of Turkish proverbs,
Sandals of proven leather,
　　A bottle of water called, yes, "Life"
In the language of the country—pine trees
　　　　stencilled on the glass.

Last Thursday you were standing by a puddle
　　　　in Istanbul asking a question:
"Why am I not home, where I should be?"
Now you're east into Asia, hearing absently
　　　　alien conjugations,
Hoping this bus won't dizzy off this mountain.

　　　　"So you think you're a fish now?"
　　　　"It's true that time is a river."
From dreaming fingers your rings dumbly witness your travels.
One hand goes to your wallet, where sober dollars
　　　　stiffly face the gaudy local bills.
Your passport is there as well,
　　　　　　establishing your identity.

　　Nod, and in the morning wake to
Acres of sunflowers
　　　　warmer than any human welcome;

Haystacks domed like the domes of whitewashed mosques,
And the Black Sea rising out of itself
like the fragrance of remoteness.

from *The New Yorker*

Kamelopard

◊   ◊   ◊

Say that the night was starred, the year not far
in advance of this, the sheik in his tent alone,
smoking his pipe. Outdoors the desert shone
in reflection of the moon that swung its arc
over the sweeping sands and the dunes' dark,
rolling shadows. Say the sound of a car

traveling the midnight highway sang its whine
the other side of the palms. The camels stirred.
The women on their pallets dreamed a bird
perched on the ridgepole, sang a single note,
then fell to silence: They heard the motor float
upon its echo, taper to the fine

edge of a dream, and finally disappear.
A thin blue haze of hashish smoke was spread
in layers about the sheik who went to bed
with fleeting images moving behind his eyes
and dropped, among his coverlets and his sighs,
into a wadi deep as any mere.

Pretend he did not know when he awoke
hearing those sounds, sat up, the lingering fumes
of his journeys bemusing him with spumes
and ebbing fountains. Say that the moaning died,
that stillness took the desert back to its wide
waters beneath a sky like spangled smoke;

say he knew certainly at last, beneath
the fabric of his life, of his abode
striping the solitude of sand and road,
that he was alone forever with the reason why
the camel is, under a blank canopy of sky,
the only herbivore with a carnivore's teeth.

from *The Formalist*

Word Silence

◇ ◇ ◇

There's a flame like the flame of fucking
that longs to be put out: words are filings
drawn toward a vast magnetic silence.
The loins ask their usual question
concerning loneliness.
The answer is always a mountaintop
erasing itself in a cloud.
It's as if the mind keeps flipping
a coin with a lullaby on one side
and a frightening thrill on the other,
and if it lands it's
back in the air at once.
A word can rub itself rosy
against its cage of context,
starting a small fire in the sentence
and trapping for a moment
the twin scents of now and goodbye.
The sexual mimicry always surprises me:
the long dive the talky mind makes
into the pleasures of its native dark.
Like pain, such joy is locked
in forgetfulness, and the prisoner
must shout for freedom again and again.
Is that what breaks the sentences apart
and spreads their embers in a cooling silence?
The pen lies in the bleach of sunlight
fallen on the desk, ghost-sheet of a bed

turned back. If I look for a long time
into its wordlessness, I can see
the vestiges of something that I knew
dissolving. Something that I no longer know.
And there I sleep like an innocent
among the words I loved
but crushed for their inflammable perfumes.

from *The Yale Review*

ROSANNA WARREN

Necrophiliac

◊   ◊   ◊

More marrow to suck, more elegies
to whistle through the digestive track. So help
me God to another dollop of death,
come on strong with the gravy and black-eyed peas,
slop it all in the transcendental stew
whose vapors rise and shine in the nostrils of heaven.
Distill the belches, preserve the drool as ink:
Death, since you nourish me, I'll flatter you
inordinately. Consumers both, with claws
cocked and molars prompt at the fresh-dug grave,
reaper and elegist, we collaborate
and batten in this strictest of intimacies,
my throat an open sepulchre, my tongue
forever groping grief forever young.

from *The Atlantic Monthly*

Eyeglasses

◇　◇　◇

Before my grandparents left Auschwitz,
they went to the enormous heap of eyeglasses,
thinking that by a miracle
they might find their own.
But it was hopeless to sift
through that mountain of tangled pairs.
They began to try on
one after another.
They had nothing
to read, so they checked
the wrinkles on their hands.
They'd bring the hand up close,
try to trace the orbits of knuckles,
the creased map of the palm.
If one eye saw right,
the other was blurred;
haze stammered the line of life.
They took several pairs.
Later in their home town
each got a prescription.
For a while they kept the other pairs;
then sighed, rubbed the smooth frames,
and threw the glasses from Auschwitz away.

My mother is embarrassed telling me the story,
embarrassed her parents took anything at all
from the piles of looted belongings.

But I'd have been like them.
I'd have taken a dozen pairs.
Those who have nothing end up
with too much, of the wrong kind.
I think of that old couple, my grandparents,
trying to read their hands
through the glasses of the dead.
Crow winter sky,
rows of empty wooden barracks.
The woman and the man
help each other up,
lean on a small handcart they found, walk on.

from *Exquisite Corpse*

C. K. WILLIAMS

The Knot

◇   ◇   ◇

Deciphering and encoding, to translate, fabricate, revise; the abstract
   star, the real star;
crossing over boundaries we'd never known were there until we found
   ourselves beyond them.
A fascination first: this was why the dream existed, so our definitions
   would be realized.
Then more than fascination as we grasped how dream could infiltrate
   the mundane with its radiance.
There'd be no mundane anymore: wholly given to the dream, our
   debilitating skepticisms overcome,
we'd act, or would be acted on—the difference, if there'd been one,
   would have been annulled—
with such purity of motive and such temperate consciousness that out-
   come would result from inspiration
with the same illumination that the notion of creation brings when
   it first comes upon us.
No question now of fabricating less ambiguous futures, no trying
   to recast recalcitrant beginnings.
It would be another empire of determination, in which all movement
   would be movement toward;
mergings, joinings, in which existence would be generated from the
   qualities of our volition;
intention flowing outward into form and back into itself in intricate
   threadings and weavings;
intuitions shaped as logically as crystal forms in rock, a linkage at the
   incandescent core:

knots of purpose we would touch into as surely as we touch the
rippling lattice of a song.

No working out of what we used to call identity, our consummations
would consist of acts,

of participating in a consciousness that wouldn't need, because it grew
from such pure need,

acknowledgment or subject: we'd be held in it, always knowing there
were truths beyond it.

Cleansed even of our appetite for bliss, we'd only want to know the
ground of our new wonder,

and we wouldn't be surprised to find that it survived where we'd
known it had to all along,

in all for which we'd blamed ourselves, repented and corrected, and
never for a moment understood.

from *Antaeus*

Winter-Worship

◇   ◇   ◇

Mother of Darkness, Our Lady,
Suffer our supplications,
                   our hurts come unto you.
Hear us from absence your dwelling place,
Whose ear we plead for.
                End us our outstay.

Where darkness is light, what can the dark be,
                     whose eye is single,
Whose body is filled with splendor
In winter,
        inside the snowflake, inside the crystal of ice
Hung like Jerusalem from the tree.

January, rain-wind and sleet-wind,
Snow pimpled and pock-marked,
               half slush-hearted, half brocade,
Under your noon-dimmed day watch,
Whose alcove we harbor in,
            whose waters are beaded and cold.

A journey's a fragment of Hell,
           one inch or a thousand miles.
Darken our disbelief, dog our steps.

Inset our eyesight,
Radiance, loom and sting,

                  whose ashes rise from the flames.

from *Field*

FRANZ WRIGHT

Depiction of Childhood

◇ ◇ ◇

After Picasso

It is the little girl
guiding the minotaur
with her free hand—
that devourer

and all the terror he's accustomed to
effortlessly emanating,
his ability to paralyze
merely by becoming present,

entranced somehow, and transformed
into a bewildered
and who knows, grateful
gentleness . . .

and with the other hand
lifting her lamp.

from *Field*

Vertumnal

◇   ◇   ◇

1

Close *call*, close *call*, close *call*: this early in the morning
The raucous crows' raw caws are ricochets off rock.

Afloat on wire from a dead tree's branch a piece of charred limb
Repeats a finch that perched on it in its last life.

Here under the pergola, loaded with green wistaria,
Misty air wistful with a few late lavender clusters.

Light falling in petal-sized spots across the notebook page
(Falling just now for instance on the phrase *Light falling*),

And under the feeder where the thumb-sized Calliope hummer
Hovers like a promising word on wings thrumming

To slip her bill-straw past the busy sugar ants
Through the red flower's grill into the sweetened red water,

And over there in your "office" under the lean-to under the crabapple,
Its fruit (like tiny ottomans) rotting sweetly on the branch

(Bouquet of Calvados and fresh tobacco),
Where in the midst of spades and pruners, hatchets, hoes, and shears,

Trowels, dibbles, rakes, and sickles you ground your axes,
Sharpened your wits, filed your notes and journals,

Moving through the garden, through all you made of where you lived—
You catch your ex-son-in-law, taking photos, figs, and notes on notes.

2

All round the garden are ghosts of what we called your "sculptures":
Pruned limbs, and broken, dried out to dove-gray, steel-gray,

Balanced, cantilevered, interlocked like skeletons
Of lovers, wrestlers, lovers; dried vines dangling

From a high branch and snaking up a makeshift bench;
A lonely felloe with its **V**s of spokes against a wall;

A lithe gnarl of live oak, grain rainwashed,
Sundrawn into shape, head cocked, curious,

Wedged in its hanging basket—as though in some square nest?
Whimsical, estranged, you left it all up in the air.

The ancient plum tree, its chief remaining limb become its trunk,
Leans on a forked crutch stuck in earth.

Eldritch, splendid in its beads of resin,
It has been dying twenty years. *Go slow*, you'd say,

On any occasion of stress or lift: *Go slow*—
Unhurried as the date palm, your family around you nervous as finches.

Weeding, staking, mulching, always with some startled kerchief
Or boxers remnant or paisley necktie binding your brow.

Things ripened. Rounded out. Entered new lives by smidgins.
By pulses. You went slow. And suddenly were gone.

Brassily proud of your descent, you still had little Polish—
And less polish. You read no poetry yet wrote a lot—

Sometimes inventing Cavafy in the rough
("We need not forget the love that was not bestowed").

Newmanian from nose to mottoes ("Growth proves life"),
Catholic existentialist, you thought all others,

Abbagnano through Zubiri, alien kindred souls—
Born thin, pedestrian, worn through—or even kindred heels.

Belligerent as Pound in his egregious master-baiting,
You scoffed at "experts," believed in nature's living art,

Like the piece of driftwood that, when stood on end,
Changed to a naked figure poised *en pointe*, a rib scooped out,

Yet couldn't leave unchanged whatever came your way.
Pie tins flashed in the olive and the fig—not to scare birds,

Either, but to catch the sun—and catch the moon.
You would have fixed the Adam on a pedestal . . . So I did.

No one would put you there. Nor were you in paradise
Alone, although you loved to be alone. And maybe now you are—

Alone with your thoughts, with galaxies, with nebulae
Slowly exploding forever behind newly opened eyes.

You cut the thorny lemon, and it cut back. Your fingers,
Cross-hatched, were thick as roots, with eyes of their own,

In queer places, like potatoes' eyes, and noses of their own,
Used as moles to breaking earth—

Densely wrinkled, blunt, penile. Well, Raymond V. Bomba,
The V for Valentine, whose day you were born on, we miss you,

Old Vertumnus. The V for *verto* and all its furcations.
And for the Virgin in the birdbath's center in the garden's

Who sees you still, the blanket hung to screen a rift in greenery,
Taking your sunbath—hunkered naked, or standing naked, a little bent.

V for the forked wand and "the poor bare forked animal."
Sorting your "effects," your wife and daughter found a clutch

Of photos clipped and cropped and pasted into thoughtful paginal
Compositions or left loose to be shuffled. A fingered muff

Matches a bearded mouth, a pinkish cock and a stiff tongue rhyme.
The edges have been tenderly rounded. (For once you cut some
        corners).

Hankering, reverent, you left them there to tell the family—what?
There in the old goat shed across from guava and kumquat . . .

Kumquat. Who would not succumb to the word, its verjuice
And blown kiss? V also for all that's venial, vernacular.

5

In the new *Romance Philology*, a title you'd have savored:
"Vegetal-Genital Onomastics in the *Libro de Buen Amor.*"

Wonderful mouthful, its palatals, its labials!
V for its g's as soft as August's livid purple figs,

So swollen in the fondling sun they have a frosty glaze.
Under the fig tree, an old pot's full of drying *cardone*,

Pappus coarse as pubic hair, with a fresh, fierce pungency,
Burst buds gone oily brown, starseeds forming in death.

Ray, you could have told us that the same root shoots
Its milky sap through *work* and *orgy* too.

You dug pits for your rakings, grounds, rinds,
Wormy peppers, tomatoes simmered on the summer vines,

And apricots galore—windfallen, slug-gnawed, earwig-bored,
Daintily painted with snailglister and bird droppings,

Or chucked by squirrels who'd take a cheeky bite
From just ripe fruit and drop the ruin at your feet.

Fruit ripe and rife, fire-dipped, as the poet put it,
And proved upon the earth. And it is still a law

That all goes in, serpentine, vatic, dreaming on the hills—
Lavender, vespid, vibrant—this evening's hills of heaven.

6

Propped on a bench against a squatting, warty stump,
A fragment of a dealer's license frame says *Santa Monica*.

Your kind of icon. Though in the Texas house you grew up in,
And kept, and opened once a year, near Beeville, where you were born,

Every surface has its Sacred Heart or crucifix,
Its holy card, or palm branch blessed with holy water, or string of
      beads.

One rosary seemed so old I rolled and warmed it in my hands
Then smelled to see if it were made indeed of crushed rose petals.

We broomed the cobwebs from the smokeshed and the washshed
And knocked the wasps' nests down from behind the jalousies.

I hacked dewberries that held the footing in a barbed embrace
And planed and sanded swollen doors so they would close.

They would not close. "We have slown down," your daughter,
Sundumb, mumbled truly—and we could hardly fasten up,

Evenings, as we lolled and mulled in that salty latitude,
That intense lassitude, mugged by the wet heat,

Longing's very weather. On your screened porch we chewed
On local sayings, spit and scratched, and stewed in our own juices.

The old Norge plugged away beside the chair where you once read.
"The dead sing out," you'd scribbled, "for are we not the dead?"

7

A pair of wild parrots startle
Up overhead and squabble off together whole-heartedly.

Here where your family had their gin and tonic talks,
And I took issue and drinks with twists on mazy walks,

African lindens flourish—exactly where I wed your daughter.
Coaxing them from cuttings, I didn't see that she lacked sun and water.

The year turned round each year with cantaloupe and plum,
Eggplant and olive, and the vowel-dark grapes of autumn

Tied to the arbor. And as it happens, the ball of twine
Has just run out you gave to us with our first vine . . .

So where am I? *Twine* . . . Mona's word, who gave us tarragon—
And gave us too, too late, a poem . . . Its purple aura gone

To ground around it, a *pointilliste's* shadow, mystical,
The jacaranda dangles pods like desiccated testicles.

The grackle, the early bird—"the *oily* one"—will get the worm
Even as it turns. The marriage went full term,

Went unpicked, then fell like you. *Marriage*, from *mari*,
Young woman, bride . . . *tried* . . . *tied* . . . as *though* to *mara*,

Bitter. The olive's argentine, then argen*tine*. *Twine, twine* . . .
Terms mean, demean . . . Ray, you'd cure the bitter fruit in brine.

8

one night a dark light shone   moon like a thinning coin   some
Roman figure   mercurial   face dimmed with radiance   out in the
garden the lemon tree's own dark bulbs shown by it showed me a way
among your labyrinthine plots of greens   on this land scorning
profits you cultivated kale and cabbage   well flesh is grass
and money too as someone puts it is just a kind of poetry   I
think you'd think he meant it's always passing on   clinking to
link like charms its users up from A to Z   or does *it* use *us* up
(grown shiny wrinkled) in its rounds   now you were passing on
were you a kind of poetry   a sheaf of notes   snap a bill or rap
a half dollar on the counter and speak the magic formula *(change
please!)* and it turns into something else   eerie   *tink-tink* of
windchimes   a hint of mint beside the molded Virgin   shoulders
rounded as the shepherd's   lambent   the green the fluent moon
dough   quarters are given   taken   given and taken   but first
they're coined   like phrases   I hope you'll see your own way
clear to these   Ray   who were (once clouds had gathered) their
solitary shaft of light

You'd "made a living" joining sounds with images—
Like the crystalline *blps* with stones thrown in the freshet

In *The Sound of Music*. Following the clever songs you spliced
("*Do*—a female deer, *re*—a drop of golden sun, *mi* . . . "),

The Trapps escaped—while you walked off unnoticed with a Golden
    Reel.
And you escaped from Fox, but not before you'd paid, with *Patton*,

With hearing failing you like headphones in *The French Connection*.
Invasions, traps that you could not evade awaited

You in your ultramontane garden, beyond the Hollywood Hills,
Where the Reel itself would serve some realer purpose.

(Its base, engraved, sat on a low bookshelf, humiliated.)
After cocktails you'd shamble down to lock the gate behind us.

Through the car window, I'd clasp your rough glove of a hand.
We'd leave you where the twilit freeway's soft white noise

Was the golden rule. Where I'd first pressed your daughter's hand.
I've sometimes thought if you had lived I'd not have let it go.

But then we must let go. It was almost as though I died
To her when you did, and as though it were you I couldn't leave—

As though somehow you'd been my father too.
As though at last without you anything were possible to do.

10

We cannot know, and yet I know you started to leave life
The way I'd later take the plane from Los Cabos:

One wasn't eager but had had enough of the guacamole
And your beloved mariachi to have standards set for ever after.

Now and again the snorkeling had been breathtaking,
That life below life, the flit of selflit fish in sunken cities,

Although one had been banged by this wave or that,
Into some rocky pocket at the reef's tip, say, and socked about,

Yet escaped, but bruised and cut, if punctually, cheaply stitched.
I think your soul had begun to hover over our quick, hungry lives

The way the scuba diver hovers over busy schools,
The way the parasailor aspires to utter silence above white beach

(Where horses dream a canter up) and drifts with scissortails
Above The Two Heads, The Bishop (Rodin's Balzac), toward The
        Point,

Where Ocean marries Sea, once and for all, day after day—
Beyond the two sides of The Beach of Love,

One on the Sea, the other steps away on the so-called Pacific,
Which is not, which is cold, and turbulent, and *Muy Peligroso.*

At picnic's end, at land's, the day comes down to ice cubes on the
        sand,
Netted in the spume, sparkling whole seconds in the setting sun.

11

A squeaking cupboard—no, the hummingbird, eking out a song,
Looking it may be for material for his nest, a matrix

Woven of hair, saliva threads, plantdown, spiderweb, and lichen,
Lichen itself already complex, alga, fungus . . .

You tried to weave it all together too—in verse, in prose—
And get it straight as well. But how could you compose

In *stanzas*, who wrote among the ferns, and feverfew in flower,
Where fennel alone could hold elaborate candelabra up?

And what could you have had to do with *argument*,
Who hardly threw a thing away and even made blue plastic

Bottle caps, immortal rubbish, seem to grow on trees?
Beyond Words you entitled the last draft

Of your ever denser, ever more desperate manuscript.
Beyond palaver, you meant, and academic poppycock,

Folderol and flourish, terms that squelch and fix—
Like chokeberry corymbs and spikes of heather.

And chickweed cyme, Jack-in-the-pulpit's spadix,
And the calla lily's, milkweed umbel,

Panicle of wild oat grass, thyrse of lilac . . .
All that malarkey, flashy as the Texas meadowlark's.

12

The house you built will go, wall by wall, to Encinada's sand.
Your garden will give way to filters, pumps, floodlights.

Where will the squirrels go to stir up their old quarrels?
Where will the gopher go, who loves a life among fig roots?

This early morning's mockingbird's a rusty screw
Coming out a half turn at a time.

With such an effort you'd twist your thoughts free.
Or on your Adler bang them deeper into mystery.

Trying to write your hard time down,
You found time writing you down first, with your own pencils,

Always growing stubbier, shavings fragrant as cumin,
Fragrant as made love, erasing their own erasers.

How you loathed "realities sustained too long—
As with the saint, who can't do anything but pray . . .

Are we not always part of something else
That also needs to live, to die, to change?"

—That from your journals with their words of orchards,
Orchards of words, their round redundance, while the breeze

Sweeps the albizzia, its easy dance redone of light and shade,
And the bottlebrush that's suddenly abuzz with bees.

from *The Yale Review*

CONTRIBUTORS'
NOTES AND
COMMENTS

JONATHAN AARON was born in Northampton, Massachusetts, in 1941. His first book was *Second Sight* (Harper & Row, 1982). His second is *Corridor* (Wesleyan/The University Press of New England, 1992). He lives in Cambridge, Massachusetts.

Of "Dance Mania," Aaron writes: "I'd always liked the sound of the name Paracelsus and wanted to put the man, whoever he was, into a poem. An old-fashioned, very silly essay about medieval religious hysteria started me thinking, and I remembered a scene from Bergman's *The Seventh Seal*. These and other associations (among them the memory of a high school prom) helped get 'Dance Mania' going. I'm pretty sure that, no matter how hard we try to be objective, we know the past through a series of subjective, not to say fictive, operations. On the other hand, some of the facts I mention in the poem are—or were—true."

AGHA SHAHID ALI was born in New Delhi in 1949 and raised in Kashmir. An assistant professor of English and creative writing at Hamilton College in upstate New York, he is the author of five collections of poetry, the most recent of which are *The Half-Inch Himalayas* (Wesleyan University Press, 1987), *A Walk Through the Yellow Pages* (SUN/gemini Press, 1987), and *A Nostalgist's Map of America* (W. W. Norton, 1991). His selected poems, *The Belovéd Witness*, will be published in India by Viking Penguin in 1992. He has also translated the major Urdu poet Faiz Ahmed Faiz; his translations, *The Rebel's Silhouette*, appeared from Peregrine Smith Books in 1991. In 1986, UMI Research Press published Agha Shahid Ali's only scholarly book, *T. S. Eliot as Editor*.

Of "I See Chile in My Rearview Mirror," Agha writes: "When Carol Houck Smith, my editor at Norton, and I were negotiating the final manuscript of *A Nostalgist's Map of America*, she suggested that I write one more Southwestern poem for the book. Several years ago I had written a poem after seeing Costa-Gavras's film *Missing*, which deals with the 1972 coup in Chile. During the recent four years, I had been thinking of writing a poem in which the central image was a giant mirror (as big as a 70mm screen) in the Sonoran desert, reflecting all of South America. When Carol suggested a new poem, somehow the poem inspired by *Missing* and the image of the giant mirror came together. As for the form of the poem, I have of late been writing poems that look formal but reveal themselves to be quite free. The first stanza of this poem occurred in an *abab* scheme, and I went with that scheme for the rest of the poem. The rhymes are sometimes exact, sometimes slant, sometimes off, and sometimes (the stringent critic may say) way-off. But I am quite delighted with my 'Utah/blue tar' rhyme."

JOHN ASH was born in Manchester, England, in 1948, and was educated at the University of Birmingham. Since 1985 he has lived in New York City. He has won grants and awards from the Ingram Merrill Foundation, the Whiting Foundation, and the Anne and Erlo Van Waveren Foundation. He has written reviews for the *New York Times Book Review*, the *Washington Post Book World*, the *Village Voice*, and *Art in America*. His books include *The Goodbyes* (1982), *The Branching Stairs* (1984), and *Disbelief* (1987), all from Carcanet. *The Burnt Pages*, a new collection of poems, was published by Random House in 1991.

Of "The Ungrateful Citizens," Ash writes: "I have always been fond of writing that describes places the writer hasn't been to. 'The Ungrateful Citizens' was a direct response to a prose poem by Max Jacob (*Littérature et Poésie*) in which a small boy tells a story about Naples. The boy's father then remarks that he has never been to Naples, to which the speaker of the poem replies, 'Sir, your child is a poet.' "

JOHN ASHBERY was born in Rochester, New York, in 1927. He is the author of thirteen books of poetry, including *Flow Chart* (Knopf, 1991), and a volume of art criticism, *Reported Sightings* (Knopf, 1989). His *Self-Portrait in a Convex Mirror* (Viking, 1975) received the Pulitzer Prize for poetry as well as the National Book

Critics Circle Award and the National Book Award. A new collection, called *Hotel Lautréamont*, is scheduled to appear in 1992. In 1989–90 he delivered the Charles Eliot Norton lectures at Harvard. He is currently Charles P. Stevenson, Jr. Professor of Languages and Literature at Bard College. He was guest editor of *The Best American Poetry 1988*.

ROBIN BEHN was born in Bay Shore, New York, in 1958. She has taught at Knox College in Galesburg, Illinois, and currently teaches in the M.F.A. program at the University of Alabama. She has received fellowships from the state arts councils of Illinois and Alabama, and from the National Endowment for the Arts. Her first book of poems, *Paper Bird* (Texas Tech, 1988), won the Associated Writing Programs Award in poetry. A second collection of poems is forthcoming from HarperCollins this year. With Chase Twichell she coedited *The Practice of Poetry: Writing Exercises from Poets Who Teach* (HarperCollins, 1992).

Of "Midwestern Villanelle," Behn writes: "Although I don't often write in fixed forms, in this case I decided to try a villanelle because I thought its demanding repetitions might help me keep moving through a field of material I felt stuck in, unable to proceed. I had had the first line for many months. But though it chanted itself, mantralike, in my brain, nothing seemed to come after it. It was a refrain without a poem. Finally, the very difficulty of proceeding became the subject of the third line, the other refrain.

"I wanted to reconstruct the odd feeling of a long-distance love affair that, though clear in its loveliness to both parties, never came to a resolution, a shortening of distance. The formalities of the villanelle made it easier to address 'you,' the absent lover—like asking a very proper aunt to hand-deliver a steamy epistle."

CHARLES BERNSTEIN was born in New York in 1950. Recent books include *A Poetics* (Harvard University Press, 1992) and, from Sun & Moon Press, *Rough Trades* (1991), *The Nude Formalism*, with Susan Bee (1989), and *The Sophist* (1987). He edited *The Politics of Poetic Form: Poetry and Public Policy* (Roof, 1990) and, with Bruce Andrews, $L = A = N = G = U = A = G = E$. He teaches in the poetics program at the State University of New York at Buffalo.

Of "How I Painted Certain of My Pictures," Bernstein writes:

"A poem should make its own experience, Uncle Hodgepodge used to say. I tend to dislike readings where the poet defines every detail and reference of the work so that by the time you get to the poem it's been reduced to an illustration of the anecdotes and explanations that preceded it. I figure if a reader or listener can't make out a particular reference or train of thought, that's okay—it's very much the way I experience things in everyday life. If the poem is at times puzzling or open-ended or merely suggestive, rather than explicit, maybe it gives readers or listeners more space for their own interpretations and imaginations. Different readers pick up different things and for any reader certain allusions are bound to be striking while others will seem opaque, but which is which changes from reader to reader. What I like in poems is encountering the unexpected and I enjoy not knowing where I am or what comes next.

"Which means I try to derail trains of thoughts as much as follow them; what you get is a mix of different types of language pieced together as in a mosaic—very 'poetic' diction next to something that sounds overheard, intimate address next to philosophical imperatives, plus a mix of would-be proverbs, slogans, jingles, nursery rhymes, songs. I love to transform idioms as much as traditional metrics because I'm looking to say things I can only say in poems; I'm driven by that necessity. Sometimes there's a gap between sentences, sometimes the sound or sentiment carries over that gap: these shifting, modulated transitions express my philosophy as much as my prosody.

"For me poetry and poetics are not so much a matter of how I can make words mean something I want to say but rather letting language find ways of meaning through me. Form is never more than an extension of sound and syntax: the music of poetry is the sound of sense coming to be in the world.

"The name of my poem is a play on Raymond Roussel's title *How I Wrote Certain of My Books*. The 'you's in the poem, by the way, refer to *you*; the *I* is harder to locate and appears to be the result of a series of 'Search and Replace' operations performed over many years."

GEORGE BILGERE was born in St. Louis, Missouri, on July 4, 1951. He currently lives in Cleveland, where he teaches in the English department at John Carroll University. Last year he taught in Spain as a Fulbright Fellow. He received a grant in poetry from the National Endowment for the Arts in 1989. His poems have appeared in *Sewanee Review*, *Chicago Review*, and *Prairie Schooner*.

Bilgere writes: " 'Healing' came about as a result of a two-year visiting professorship I spent at the University of Oklahoma. Although I grew up on the West Coast and had spent very little time in that part of the country, I was strongly attracted to it. The huge expanses of open plains, the turbulent weather, the accent, the leaning toward fundamentalist modes of religious expression, the relatively unhurried pace of life in a small town, were all aspects of Oklahoma that I found tremendously appealing after my frenetic years in Los Angeles. I wanted the poem to reflect the life I found there with its pathos, its beauty, its earnestness, its weird incongruities, in a way I hoped would be not condescending but affectionate. And I think the poem also reveals something about me as a kind of. itinerant American, always traveling, looking with longing and nostalgia, unable somehow to quite enter the worlds I find myself passing through. Finally, I would say that the poem is about failure, and the human ability to find consolation among the debris of our small disasters."

ELIZABETH BISHOP (1911–1979) was born in Worcester, Massachusetts, and died in Boston. When she was eight months old, her father died; four years later, her mother suffered a complete mental breakdown. As a child, she lived with her mother's family in Great Village, Nova Scotia, with her father's parents in Worcester, and with a maternal aunt in Boston. She graduated from Vassar in 1934 and lived in New York, Paris, Key West, Mexico, Washington, D.C. (as Consultant in Poetry at the Library of Congress from 1949 until 1951) and, for nearly twenty years, in Rio de Janeiro, Petrópolis, and Ouro Prêto, Brazil. Her books include *North & South* (1946); *Poems: North & South—A Cold Spring* (1955, Pulitzer Prize); *Questions of Travel* (1965); *The Complete Poems* (1969, National Book Award), and *Geography III* (1976). She also translated *The Diary of "Helena Morley"* (1957), wrote, "with the editors of *Life*," the Life World Library *Brazil* (1962), and coedited *An Anthology of Twentieth-Century Brazilian Poetry* (1972). Her posthumous volumes include *The Complete Poems 1927–1979* (Farrar, Straus & Giroux, 1983) and *The Collected Prose*, edited by Robert Giroux

(Farrar, Straus & Giroux, 1984). A volume of her selected letters is now being edited by Robert Giroux.

Elizabeth Bishop's poem beginning "Dear, my compass" appeared in Lloyd Schwartz's article "Elizabeth Bishop and Brazil" in *The New Yorker*, September 30, 1991. Schwartz discovered the poem in a little inn in Ouro Prêto, the eighteenth-century mountain town in Brazil where Elizabeth Bishop bought a house in 1965.

Schwartz writes: "Here is the unmistakable voice of Elizabeth Bishop; here the fairy-tale vividness and coloring-book clarity of the images (the product of what Robert Lowell once called her 'famous eye'); the geographical references—and restlessness—of the world traveler; the delicate yet sharply etched jokes, often at her own expense ('Protestants, and / heavy drinkers': she was both); the apparent conversational casualness disguising the formality of the versification; the understated yet urgent sexuality; even the identification with animals. 'I believe in the oblique, the indirect approach,' she wrote in the voice of a Strayed Crab.

"She never published this untitled poem. She abandoned it in Brazil. And, with typical obliqueness, it is even *about* Brazil—or, rather, what Brazil is not. She must have been living there for more than a decade when she wrote it, probably in the mid-nineteen-sixties, and of the poems she wrote there it is the only one—at least, the only one that has come to light—in which she weighs the world of her childhood in Nova Scotia against the life she chose for herself later, in which she measures not only how far she has traveled from her origins but how difficult it is to escape them."

Lloyd Schwartz is codirector of the creative writing program at the University of Massachusetts in Boston. He also serves as the classical music editor of the *Boston Phoenix* and the classical music critic on National Public Radio's *Fresh Air*. He is the author of *"That Sense of Constant Re-adjustment": Elizabeth Bishop's* North and South (Garland, 1987) and coeditor of *Elizabeth Bishop and Her Art* (University of Michigan Press, 1983). In 1990 and 1991, the United States Information Agency invited him to lecture on Elizabeth Bishop and to teach contemporary American poetry in Brazil. Lloyd Schwartz's most recent book of poems is *Goodnight, Gracie* (University of Chicago Press, 1992).

ROBERT BLY was born in Madison, Minnesota, in 1926. He lives with his wife Ruth in Minneapolis and makes a living by writing, lecturing, and reading. His most recent book is *American Poetry: Wildness and Domesticity*, gathering his essays on American poetry of recent decades. "The Crippled Godwit" will be included in his collected prose poems available in 1992 from HarperCollins under the title *What Have I Ever Lost by Dying?* The paperback edition of his book *Iron John* appeared in 1992 from Vintage.

Of "The Crippled Godwit," Bly writes: "The godwit poem was written on the Pacific Beach at Asilomar near Point Lobos, during a break in a seminar I was teaching there on the theme of Calcinatio in medieval alchemy, but the poem doesn't seem to be connected with that at all. It began in admiration of the beauty of the godwits, and how marvelously they are adapted to the sea edge that they live on. I got a shock when I realized how long it took me to see the one wounded godwit. That I saw it at all is probably due to the loneliness I felt that weekend living among strangers."

LUCIE BROCK-BROIDO was born and raised in Pennsylvania. Her first collection of poems, *A Hunger*, was published by Knopf in 1988. Educated at Johns Hopkins University and Columbia University, she has held a fellowship from the Fine Arts Work Center in Provincetown, the Hoyns Fellowship from the University of Virginia, a Massachusetts Artist's Fellowship, and a grant from the National Endowment for the Arts. She lives in Cambridge, Massachusetts, and is the Briggs-Copeland Assistant Professor in Poetry at Harvard University.

Of "Inevitably, She Declined," Brock-Broido writes: "Since Day One, I've been in love with the Idea of Anne Boleyn; she keeps appearing in visitations in my work. When Henry VIII fell in love with the idea of Anne Boleyn, an entire country changed its faith to accommodate this affair. In January 1533, Henry made Anne his second Queen consort.

"After one thousand or so days, the romance ruined; Anne was convicted of adultery & beheaded at the Tower of London on 19 May 1536. Anne had failed to produce a male heir for the King. Her fatal flaw was in producing for Henry—a girl. The *she* of 'Inevitably, She Declined,' is Elizabeth, only offspring of Henry & Anne, Queen of England & Ireland from 1558 to 1603.

"I was reading a documentary life of William Shakespeare, & came across these lines: *While folk in Stratford went about the ordinary affairs of life, great events were taking place on the national stage. Inevitably, the Queen declined. She had ruled for almost half a century . . . Towards the end a heavy dullness & irritability, the infirmities of advanced age, overtook her . . .*

"At the age of seventy, in her bishop's chair (there was no Death *Bed* scene; so certain she would never rise again, she refused to lie down), Elizabeth sat to wait out her finity. Her wedding ring, symbolizing her marriage to England (her *only* marriage; she chose to reign her kingdom husbandless), was, of necessity, filed from her finger, so embedded was it in her flesh after nearly fifty years. On 24 March 1603, she expired; bonfires blazed in London's streets. This was the last day of the Tudor dynasty.

"As is often the case in my case, the poem was born of its title—it all seemed inevitable to me—the Declining, the She, the Inevitability of the She's decline. I had the heats of history, a narrative, an ostensible purpose, a politic— & I chose to crowd all these heats into the densest song. So I concocted the whole Ordeal in the sonnet form, bending the form, Carrying On in the hellish embrace of the confines of the fourteen lines. The sonnet— a marriage of Hysteria & Haiku (definition attributed, to my knowledge, to the poet Bruce Smith)— seemed the perfect crowded Room for the overwrought, swollen, declining, bedecked, embellished story of Elizabeth— bastard of Henry, girl-child, *Idea*— of Anne."

JOSEPH BRODKSY was born in Leningrad in 1940 and came to the United States in 1972, an involuntary exile from the Soviet Union. His books of poetry available in English include *A Part of Speech* (1980) and *To Urania* (1988), both from Farrar, Straus & Giroux. His book of essays, *Less Than One* (Farrar, Straus & Giroux, 1986), won the National Book Critics Circle Award for criticism. In 1987 Joseph Brodsky was awarded the Nobel Prize for literature. He is currently Andrew Mellon Professor of Literature at Mount Holyoke College. A translation of his first play, *Marbles*, was published by Farrar, Straus & Giroux in 1989, and a second play, *Democracy!*, has been performed in several European cities and is scheduled for production in Washington, D.C. He became the poet laureate of the United States in 1991.

HAYDEN CARRUTH was born and raised in rural Connecticut, lived in Chicago and New York, then for twenty years in northern Vermont, and now resides in upstate New York. He recently retired from Syracuse University, where he had taught in the graduate creative writing program. He has published twenty-seven books, chiefly poetry but also including a novel, three books of criticism, and two anthologies. His most recent books are *Tell Me Again How the White Heron Rises and Flies Across the Nacreous River at Twilight Toward the Distant Islands* (New Directions, 1989) and *The Sleeping Beauty*, revised edition (Copper Canyon Press, 1990). His *Collected Shorter Poems, 1946–1991* will be published in the spring of 1992 (Copper Canyon Press). He has been the editor of *Poetry*, poetry editor of *Harper's*, and for twenty years an advisory editor of *The Hudson Review*. In 1988 he was appointed a senior fellow by the National Endowment for the Arts.

Of "Sex," Carruth writes: " 'Sex' was written about four years ago in the winter of 1987. For a couple of years it was lost, but then turned up among other papers from that time. I wrote my first poem about impotence more than fifteen years ago, I think, when I was fifty-three or so. I've written others. Now I'm seventy, still sexually active, and I expect to continue to be; but the changes are unmistakable, too, and not easy to take. I don't see other people writing about impotence. I wonder why? To me sex in all its aspects has always been extremely important, equal on the personal plane to justice on the social plane, and I will continue to write about it as long as I can."

BILLY COLLINS was born in New York City in 1941. He is the author of four books of poetry, the two most recent being *The Apple That Astonished Paris* (University of Arkansas Press, 1988) and *Questions About Angels* (William Morrow, 1991), a National Poetry Series selection by Edward Hirsch. He has received fellowships from the National Endowment for the Arts and the New York Foundation for the Arts and the Bess Hokin Prize from *Poetry*. He was educated at Holy Cross College and the University of California at Riverside. He is currently professor of English at Lehman College (CUNY) and lives in northern Westchester County.

Of "Nostalgia," Collins writes: "This poem is a bit like what the great hipster Lord Buckley used to call a 'wig bubble,' that is, a notion you inflate with your imagination, blowing it up to extravagant proportions. The poem began as a playful satire on the phenomenon of public nostalgia, the kind that insists we all should share some sweet regret over the passing of a decade. As far as I know, this is a strictly twentieth-century and very American mannerism; indeed, it begins at the very turn of the century with the figment of the 'gay nineties.' 'Nostalgia' pokes fun at nostalgia by extending it ridiculously into the historical past and by shifting it to a European context. Oddly, this poem began with its first line—'Remember the 1340's?'—which points the poem in a definite direction and opens up the kinds of possibilities I am quick to exploit. When I follow a formula like this in a poem, I am always looking for the point when the poem wants to surprise me by swerving off in a new direction or developing an unexpected interest. What develops here is the growing prominence of the speaker himself whose dismay with the present moment is absurd yet acute nonetheless. When we finally arrive at this present with its garden of flowers and bees, we have simply reached the destination that the poem was seeking all along. I like poems that lead you by the hand to imaginary places, as children's stories do, then leave you there, a little disoriented, a long way from your native Kansas, with only a small dog at your heels."

ROBERT CREELEY was born in Arlington, Massachusetts, in 1926. After much travel he settled in Buffalo, New York, where he has taught for many years at the State University of Buffalo. He is currently the director of the poetics program there. His recent books include *Autobiography* (Hanuman Books, 1990) and *Selected Poems* (University of California Press, 1991).

Of "Other," Creeley writes: "Laurence Goldstein, editor of the *Michigan Quarterly Review*, had asked me unexpectedly to consider submitting a poem for an issue on 'The Female Body.' 'Other'—together with one written just after, 'Body'—was my response. ('Body,' which was published in *MQR*, concludes my *Selected Poems*. Written in classic quatrains, it wryly if insistently applies to all 'bodies' the same inexorable measure.) In 'Other,' the preoccupation seems to be with all that the 'body' has determined for me as well as how I've presumed or thought of it. The poem's form is a twelve-line block, felt as a sonnetlike compaction, using much resonance, imploding rhymes, a pattern that keeps returning to where it seemingly has begun. I first used it when living in Finland in 1988–89, and the most simply found instance of my preoccupation is 'Helsinki Window' (also to be found in *Selected Poems*)."

KATHLEEN DE AZEVEDO was born in Rio de Janeiro, Brazil, in 1955. She has lived most of her life in rural towns in California and in San Francisco. She is currently an M.F.A. writing candidate at the University of Washington. Her poetry has appeared in *Sojourner, Visions International*, and *A Fine Madness*. Her fiction has appeared in *The Raven Chronicles, Brooklyn Review, Reed Magazine*, and *Dream In A Minor Key*, an anthology of magic realism.

Of "Famous Women—Claudette Colbert," de Azevedo writes: "I worked as an actress, costumer, and playwright for many years. Looking back, I realize that both the enchantment and the disillusionment of working in a business that promotes fantasy played an important part in my growth as a person and as a writer. The first 'dream of success' is a part of our youth. To start over after failing the initial dream is a part of our maturing process. The day I turned down a pivotal job as a costume buyer, there was a stack of mannequins piled in the scene shop waiting to be returned to a Los Angeles costume rental agency."

CARL DENNIS was born in St. Louis in 1939. He now lives in Buffalo, where he teaches in the English department of the State University of New York. A recipient of a Guggenheim Fellowship and a grant from the National Endowment for the Arts, he has written six books of poetry, most recently *Meetings with Time*, which was published by Viking in 1992.

Of "Spring Letter," Dennis writes: "I was hoping here to write a lament that is also a celebration, combining the feelings of diminishment and enlargement, and linking them to a particular place, half found, half made."

DEBORAH DIGGES was born in Jefferson City, Missouri, in 1950. Her first book of poems, *Vesper Sparrows* (Atheneum, 1986), won the Delmore Schwartz Memorial Poetry Prize. A second collection,

Late in the Millennium (Knopf), appeared in 1989. *Fugitive Spring*, a memoir, also from Knopf, has just been published. A recent fellow of the National Endowment for the Arts, the Guggenheim Foundation, and others, Digges has taught in the graduate writing divisions of New York and Columbia universities. She is an assistant professor of English at Tufts University.

Of "My Amaryllis," Digges writes: "One Christmas, instead of the dreaded fruitcake, my parents sent me an amaryllis bulb. I followed the enclosed instructions, and sure enough, by February, the bulb had sprouted so beautiful a white flower, I suspected genetic engineering. It grew to be nearly four feet high and dominated my dining room—a cold room, really, with uncovered windows on three sides, each looking out on Boston's typically bleak urban landscape. In that context the amaryllis was so touchingly natural, so vulnerable and brave, I had the sense I could warm my hands over it. When over my fortieth birthday it began to lean, its blossoms, just at the edges, tinted brown, I wrote the poem. I think of it, then, as a sort of pact with the Fates."

STEPHEN DUNN was born in Forest Hills, N.Y., in 1939. He teaches at Stockton State College, where he is Trustee Fellow in the Arts. "Smiles" appeared in his eighth collection of poetry, *Landscape at the End of the Century* (W. W. Norton, 1991).

Of "Smiles," Dunn writes: "When I moved to South Jersey seventeen years ago, I was struck by the phrase *Black Horse Pike*, and wanted to put it in a poem. It's the road that runs from Atlantic City to Philadelphia, a road I often travel. Gradually I became inured to those words as to, for example, the *Walt Whitman Bridge*. The poem got started because I remembered that I loved the sound and the resonance of Black Horse Pike, which keyed a series of remembrances and fictions."

SUSAN FIRER was born in Milwaukee in 1948. Currently she teaches creative writing at the University of Wisconsin at Milwaukee. She has one book out with New Rivers Press, and a second book, titled *The Underground Communion Rail*, is due out from West End Press in 1992.

Firer writes: " 'The Bright Waterfall of Angels' was written from place and gender and need. In it I'm trying to write the poetic world around me from my corner Chinese restaurant to Lake Michigan. I share Neruda's belief in an impure poetry, one soiled and stained with our 'shameful behavior . . . vigils and dreams . . . declarations of loathing, love . . . and beasts.' I'm trying to take Anne Sexton's dare to tell it true. In 'The Bright Waterfall of Angels' I'm having a whack at all that while I explore what I do know and what I don't know. 'As a writer one has to take the chance on being a fool,' says Sexton, and I hope I'm risking that, too."

ALICE FULTON was born in Troy, New York, in 1952. Her books include *Powers of Congress* (Godine, 1990), *Palladium* (University of Illinois Press, 1986), and *Dance Script with Electric Ballerina* (University of Pennsylvania Press, 1983). She has received fellowships from the John T. and Catherine D. MacArthur Foundation, the Guggenheim Foundation, and the Ingram Merrill Foundation. Her work was also included in the 1988, 1989, and 1991 editions of *The Best American Poetry*. Currently, she is an associate professor of English at the University of Michigan, Ann Arbor.

Fulton writes: " 'A Little Heart-to-Heart with the Horizon' was written around Thanksgiving 1990, when I had a few days off from teaching. I live on an old farm in the Midwest, where there's no shortage of horizon. Without the criblike enclosure of buildings, you get a good look at that fine seam. Without hills, mesas, or mountains making their iconographic WOW against the sky, the horizon is both subtle and plentiful. As an odd consequence, you don't much notice it. Here and there the hem unravels into a tiny turbulence of trees. I wrote the poem between staring at the local brink of things and watching U.S. troops on the news. The army was stationed in the Saudi Arabian desert where the horizon's sharp as a bayonet. That hard line made the edge of the Midwest look fuzzy. The peripheral and the central have their own little war within the poem, which gradually formed around spatial, hierarchical tropes: the flat and low (horizon, desert, sheets, Michigan, fields, anchor); the vertical or high (clouds, heavens, derricks, summit, figure).

"Although I mostly floundered along without knowing what the words would come to, one of my conscious aims was to combine a casual American diction with the singing qualities of the high lyric mode. I wanted each line to be textured and tight, but I also hoped for the accurate, effortless soaring I value in a singer's voice. These aims—for ease and for density—seem to be in opposition. The challenge was to walk a line wedding each to each.

"I'm particularly interested in how a poem moves the reader through language: its degree and means of impulsion. I love poetry that moves well. (I offer these tastes not as essentialist aesthetic truths, but as personal preferences.) To me, 'moving well' entails a combination of rhythmic repetition and surprise. A poem with too much equilibrium won't hold my interest. I need the occasional twist, lift, curve, jaggedness. There's an ineluctable quality to a regular meter, which pleases by fulfilling expectations of what comes next. On the other hand, rhythms that can't be anticipated offer a marvelous improvisatory quality, like jazz. I tend to like poetry that combines these two ways of pleasing the ear: the sure-footedness of regular meters tripped by the occasional, wayward prosodic move: an iambic fluidity punctured by oddly placed, strong caesuras, say, or jazzed by repeated downbeats of spondees. The combination of wish fulfillment (as found in the regular grace of iambs) and unsettling musical turns keeps me moving through the poem. I also try to use the dynamic properties of rhythm and line to slow or hasten the reader's progress. Thus, in my poem a line of iambic trimeter, 'in your repose, a balance,' is followed by a line composed of one spondee: 'beam, point.' To my ear, the solid, spondaic BAM, BAM punctuates, punctures, and puts the brakes on iambic gracefulness, briefly.

"I find in this poem the wish to be both anchored and adrift, earthly and heavenly, held and released, breathing and breathless. So often humans seem the intrusive presence in an otherwise unself-conscious natural world. At the end the poem takes an epistemolog-ical turn. What's a self-aware body to do? To feel and know that we feel, to notice and give notice, to reflect upon a world that can't reflect on itself—I'll say one thing: it gives us something to do. The poem also puns on the human wish to stand up and signify, to bisect circumference and be visible. The steel I-beam of the ego: Go figure."

TESS GALLAGHER was born in Port Angeles, Washington. She lives there still, on the Strait of Juan de Fuca. She has held the Willard and Lois Mackey Chair for Poetry and Fiction at Beloit College. Her most recent poetry publications are *Moon Crossing Bridge* (Graywolf Press, 1992) and *Portable Kisses* (Capra Press, 1992). Her stories, *The Lover of Horses* (Graywolf Press, 1992), have recently been translated into Japanese and Swedish. Her essays on poetry, collected in *A Concert of Tenses* (University of Michigan Press, 1986), speak about her life growing up in the Pacific Northwest as the oldest of five children in a family where both mother and father worked at logging.

Of "We're All Pharaohs When We Die," Gallagher writes: "Like many children, I had a great love affair with picture books of Egyptian burial tombs. A central metaphor in the poem concerns the beautifully painted sarcophagi of Egyptian royalty. Words themselves are also a kind of stylized image on the spiritual container of both the poem and, more importantly, memory itself. There is a kind of reversal at the poem's end, which, if it succeeds, actually places the reader inside the sarcophagus of this poem, outside of which the almost supernatural presences of the deer gaze through a kind of membrane at the strange human world. The poem was written in memory of Raymond Carver."

AMY GERSTLER was born in San Diego, California, in 1956. She works as a freelance journalist, art critic, and teacher, and lives in Los Angeles. In 1990, her book *Bitter Angel* (North Point Press, 1990) received the National Book Critics Circle Award in poetry. She is currently working on a novel.

Of "On Wanting to Grow Horns," Gerstler writes: "Because one of the ways I support myself is by writing about art, I was lucky enough to stumble into a gallery show by Tom Knechtel, a visual artist whose work amazed me. I wrote a review of the show for an art magazine, but having been given a mere five hundred words to write about this artist's work within the confines of a conventional art review was frustrating, and seemed inadequate to express how powerful an effect the work had on me. Set in motion by Knechtel's fascinating collision of highly sexualized flora and fauna, I tried to use some of what the work stirred up in me about being torn between being human and animal, if there's any difference."

JACK GILBERT was born in Pittsburgh. His first book, *Views of Jeopardy*, won the 1962 Yale Younger Poets Prize. *Monolithos: Poems, 1962 and 1982* was published by Knopf in 1982. He has lived in Greece, Paris, Japan, and Italy, and he currently lives in western Massachusetts. "Voices Inside and Out" appeared in an issue of *Ploughshares* devoted to "The Literature of Ecstasy," edited by Gerald Stern. Gilbert's contributor's note reads as follows: "Happily writing poems. Thinking about love and poetry and teaching. Wondering whether ecstasy misses the point by being instead of." He has just finished a new book of poems.

Of "Voices Inside and Out," Gilbert writes: "I have been more and more puzzled by the lack of substantiality in the lives now of both well-educated and well-to-do Americans (who have achieved everything dreamed of and aspired to in the last ten thousand years). I look at Tucson and San Francisco and Seattle with the sense of magnitude built into me by growing up in what was then a medieval Pittsburgh. The poem is part of trying to think about that."

LOUISE GLÜCK was born in New York City in 1943. She teaches at Williams College and lives in Plainfield, Vermont. Her sixth collection, *The Wild Iris*, will be published in 1992 by Ecco Press.

Glück writes: " 'Vespers' was one of eight poems written in the summer of 1990, the first poems I'd done in nearly two years. It didn't please me much; nothing in that group pleased me much. The poems were an argument with the divine; they seemed simultaneously incomplete and a dead end—too pat, too expert, a little warmed over, limited by cleverness.

"Context has modified my assessment: 'Vespers' has become part of a book, its facility sabotaged (I hope) by the poems around it, poems written, in the summer of 1991, with a kind of wild ease for which my life affords no precedent. The risk of the unchecked ecstatic is tedium: 'Vespers' borrows the depth it lacks from the poems around it and, for its part, grounds those poems in something recognizable.

"My reservations about this poem as a single thing remain intact."

JILL GONET was born in New Bedford, Massachusetts, in 1960. Since 1985 she has lived in Seattle. Poems from her manuscript *No House Left* appear in the *Antioch Review*, *Ploughshares*, *ZYZZYVA*, *Ironwood*, and the *Black Warrior Review*.

Gonet writes: " 'Body Will' began as doodles in a notebook. I was drawing cartoons of objects that we say have body parts (a stove has a belly, a comb has teeth, and so forth). Then the idea came for a poem that would explore the location of the body in the everyday objects around us.

"About two years previously, I had been reading Villon, and loved the poem in which he facetiously bequeaths his riches to friends—riches he of course didn't have.

"Somehow the two ideas merged, and I wrote a poem that bequeaths parts of my body to the idioms that seemed they could use them. Villon willed riches he didn't have, and so do I."

JORIE GRAHAM was born in New York City in 1950. She teaches at the University of Iowa. Her most recent volume of poems, *Region of Unlikeness*, was published by the Ecco Press in 1991. She is also the author of three other volumes of poetry, *Hybrids of Plants and of Ghosts* (Princeton, 1980), *Erosion* (Princeton, 1983), and *The End of Beauty* (Ecco, 1987). She was guest editor of *The Best American Poetry 1990*.

Of "Manifest Destiny," Jorie Graham writes: "I don't know if this has much to do with the poem as it stands, but Fabrice Helion was my first lover, and when I received news of his death (an apparent suicide) by drug overdose, I happened to be unpacking books I'd kept in storage for twenty-two years—many of them inscribed to me by him—tattered Gallimard editions of German and French philosophers. Notes in my fifteen-year-old hand (in French) all over Marx and Engels and Spinoza and Schopenhauer and Kierkegaard and Nietzsche took me aback—especially the earnestness and seriousness of them, and the great, helplessly imperial desire to *know* inscribed in them tonally. As I was holding these books in my hand—reading the notes in his eighteen-year-old hand alongside mine (corrective, instructive)—the phone rang with the news of his death. All of our time together had been in Rome during my early and midteens. He was shooting heroin on and off then. In case anyone should care, the restaurant and bar in question are *Il Bolognese* and *Rosati*—then rather inexpensive. The opening scene takes place on a dirt road in Wyoming where, driving to town, I recalled the rest. As far as I can tell, it's all, though layered over time, true."

ALLEN GROSSMAN was born in Minneapolis in 1932. He is currently the Mellon Professor in the Humanities at Johns Hopkins University, Baltimore, Maryland. His most recent books are *The Ether Dome and Other Poems, New and Selected* (New Directions, 1991) and *The Sighted Singer: Two Works on Poetry for Writers and Readers* (Johns Hopkins University Press, 1991).

Grossman writes: "The sequence 'Poland of Death,' of which this poem is part, tells the history of the world as the story of the return of souls to their 'right place' in the cosmos. In this poem, 'Poland of Death (IV),' the son meets his father in the 'right place' of the father's death, to which the father has come after death by means of his own labor. The poem is composed in such a way as to present two actions: 1) The passing from father to son of the tool of the father's labor, the 'nail'; 2) The writing by the son (on behalf of the father) of the father's sentence, 'The Lord is One.' "

MARILYN HACKER was born in the Bronx in 1942. She is the author of seven books of poetry, most recently *Going Back to the River* (Random House, 1990) and *The Hang-Glider's Daughter: New and Selected Poems* (Onlywomen Press, London, 1990). She received the National Book Award in poetry for *Presentation Piece* in 1975. She divides her time between New York's Upper West Side, the Marais district in Paris, and Gambier, Ohio, where she is editor of the *Kenyon Review*.

Of "Elysian Fields," Hacker writes: "The poem is a fairly straightforward view of what's in my front yard, or one of them. Occasionally, I'm one of the morning cappuccino drinkers, with the *Times* or a yellow legal pad, fortunate enough to have a choice of comfortable interior settings where I can think about the present and the past, or read the understatement of some new disaster. I can't be *indoors* in New York these days without a painful sense of privileged humility."

DONALD HALL, who was born in Connecticut in 1928, makes his living in New Hampshire as a free-lance writer. His book-length poem, *The One Day* (Ticknor & Fields, 1988), won the National Book Critics Circle Prize in poetry; *Old and New Poems* followed from the same publisher in 1990. In summer 1992 he brought out *Their Ancient Glittering Eyes* (Ticknor & Fields), which expanded and revised his *Remembering Poets* of 1978. He was guest editor of *The Best American Poetry 1989*.

Hall writes: "Five or six years ago I heard myself scorning a currently common sort of poem: personal anecdotes in flat language that recollected feelings. I decried 'home movies' so strongly that (I realized) I desperately wanted to try them out. 'Spring Glen Grammar School' is three of them."

DANIEL HALPERN was born in Syracuse, New York, in 1945. He is the author of six collections of poetry, including *Tango, Seasonal Rights,* and *Life Among Others,* all published by Viking Penguin, and most recently, *Foreign Neon,* published by Knopf in 1991. He is the editor of *Antaeus* and the Ecco Press. He has edited *The American Poetry Anthology* (Avon, 1975), *The Art of the Tale: An International Anthology of Short Stories* (Viking Penguin, 1986), *Writers on Artists* and *On Nature,* both from North Point Press. He is coauthor of a cookbook, *The Good Food: Soups, Stews, and Pastas* (Viking Penguin, 1985), and recently published a travel book, *Halpern's Guide to the Essential Restaurants of Italy* (Addison-Wesley, 1990). His awards include a Guggenheim Fellowship and a grant from the National Endowment for the Arts. He teaches in the graduate writing program of Columbia University.

Of "Infidelities," Halpern writes: "The ever-energetic imagination yearns to partake of different lives, step out of one life to sample another. 'Infidelities' is a meditation of the imagination, composed of nonuniform shards of memory and projected fantasy, a series that participates in acts of betrayal—that is, a betrayal of *the way things are.* To say you wish to experience something *different* is to suggest discontent with the something that has been and still is—an infidelity, imagined or not. The imagination by its very nature creates unfaithful acts against what we like to call reality, and it is the intent of this poem to celebrate that violation."

ROBERT HASS was born in San Francisco, California, in 1941. He currently teaches at the University of California at Berkeley. His most recent book of poems is *Human Wishes* (Ecco, 1989). He has also cotranslated several volumes of the poems of Czeslaw Milosz, most recently *Provinces* (Ecco, 1991).

Hass writes: " 'My Mother's Nipples' began when I overheard a friend propose that subject to someone else. We were in the mountains in a restaurant in the summertime. My first thought was to make fun of the idea, my second was of the painfulness of it. These suggested a form."

VICKI HEARNE was born in Austin, Texas, in 1946. She lives in Westbrook, Connecticut, trains dogs for a living, and is a visiting fellow at the Yale Institution for Social and Policy Studies. Her books of verse are *Nervous Horses* (University of Texas, 1980) and *In the Absence of Horses* (Princeton, 1984). She has written a novel, *The White German Shepherd* (Atlantic Monthly Press, 1988). Her nonfiction includes *Adam's Task: Calling Animals By Name* (Knopf, 1986; Vintage, 1987) and *Bandit: Dossier of a Dangerous Dog* (HarperCollins, 1991). She is married to the philosopher Robert Tragesser.

Of "St. Luke Painting the Virgin," Hearne writes: "Being mostly a denizen of the deserts of the Southwest, I discovered museums at a fairly advanced age, and so was bowled over when I came across this painting in the Boston Museum of Fine Arts. The hazards it meditates on, of being dangerously entranced by divine light, were real to me the two days I spent visiting the painting. I visited it over and over. I would go look at it, then escape across the way to a dim coffee shop, write bits of the poem, and then return and look at the painting again, to find that the hazards continued to be real.

"For some reason I am now unclear about, I ended up paying admission every time I went back in, which seemed only right and natural, though my friends tell me it was idiotic, since you are given a button when you enter and you just have to show your button to get back in."

JUAN FELIPE HERRERA was born in Fowler, California, in 1948. Currently he teaches a creative writing workshop as well as drama and culture studies for the Chicano Latin American Studies Department at California State University at Fresno. He lives with his wife, the poet Margarita Luna Robles, and his two children in Fresno. He has held various writing fellowships including two grants from the National Endowment for the Arts, a Breadloaf Alan Collins Fellowship, and four California Arts Council awards. His books include *Rebozos of Love* (Tolteca Publications, 1974), *Exiles of Desire* (Arte Publico Press, University of Houston, 1985), *Facegames* (Dragon Cloud Press, 1987/ Before Columbus American Book Award), and *Akrilica* (Alcatraz Editions, 1989). He is a graduate of the Iowa Writers' Workshop.

Herrera writes: " 'Iowa Blues Bar Spiritual' comes from an invitation to go to an evening of hard music in Cedar Rapids, Iowa, while I was doing my M.F.A. in Iowa City. A friend, Tom Lutz, a cool member of the Geoff Becker Band, invited me and my wife Margarita. At odds with things I chose to stay home and peer out at the night. Somehow I got caught up with the feeling and landscape of the blues bar. I had to write about it even though I was absent. I called upon familiar and distant faces. I conjured pieces of the past, came up against tombstones, mirrors and tattoos and somehow found the little, tilted cabin lit up and open to the winds. Lutz had mentioned playing in the bars and how the band would get requests from the audience; Ritchie Valens was a favorite.

"For me the process of writing a poem has to do with heat; a firing-up of the body. There is a slippage between dream, reality and the erotic magnets dangling from the cosmos and the earth. If I can find the coordinates in the instance of a leaf-shaped call of sax and guitar riffs, I am ready."

EDWARD HIRSCH was born in Chicago in 1950 and educated at Grinnell College and the University of Pennsylvania. He has published three books of poems: *For the Sleepwalkers* (Knopf, 1981), *Wild Gratitude* (Knopf, 1986), which won the National Book Critics Circle Award, and *The Night Parade* (Knopf, 1989). He teaches at the University of Houston.

Of "Man on a Fire Escape," Hirsch writes: "This poem is an attempt to explore the literal and metaphorical possibilities of its dramatic situation: a man on a fire escape on a late day in the empire. There are a couple of things I had it in mind to do. To send a man out of his empty room onto iron stairs overlooking a city, and then to reel him back in. To describe a moment that is both ordinary and extraordinary, inside and outside of time. To invoke dusk, the hour of changes, as vividly as possible. To imagine and dwell upon an extended apocalyptic moment, the world being destroyed, and then to see that visionary moment transfigured and withdrawn, the twilight seeping into evening, the world continuing on as before. What has the man seen and what has he envisioned? Nothing. That resonating answer bears the full burden of meaning in the poem."

DANIEL HOFFMAN, born in New York in 1923, is the author of nine books of poetry. The most recent, *Hang-Gliding from Helicon: New and Selected Poems* (Louisiana State University Press, 1988), won the Paterson Poetry Prize for 1989. His book–length poem *Brotherly Love* (Random House, 1982) provides the libretto for Ezra Laderman's forthcoming oratorio of the same title.

Of "Identities," Hoffman writes: "I've just spent a year abroad. That required identity papers, many with photographs, to enter a country, stay more than six months, register with the police, drive a car, use a book in the British Library or borrow one from any of five other collections, buy a rail pass, and so on. But whose likeness validates these documents?

"Just as the British government has a shadow cabinet, each minister haunted by his rival from the opposition who combats his policies, counters his edicts, debates his proposals, so with the body politic of the psyche. Who is the shadow, who the self? Over the years I've written several poems dramatizing this sense, so widely shared, of a doppelganger within. The present poem exaggerates, satirizes, parodies the dispositions by which opposites define themselves and each other. The self may in truth be one, or the other, or it may exist somewhere in the spaces between them.

"Naturally none of these schematic afterthoughts occurred in the course of writing. The poem came as images paired, rough couplets their natural habitat, where rhyme would cancel their oppositions but alliterations, less obvious, could bring out the binary sympathies between them. First came an image of an endlessly frustrated seeking, linked somehow to rooms surrendering secrets at the turning of a single key. The challenge, to get from those to another pair that proposed life as inexorably predetermined as a computer program, and imagination owning the strength to stitch the universe together, the moon its needle's eye."

JOHN HOLLANDER was born in New York City in 1929. He has published fifteen books of poetry here and abroad, the most recent being *Harp Lake* (Knopf, 1988) and an expanded edition of his earlier *Types of Shape* (Yale University Press, 1990). He is the author of several books of criticism and theory, including *Melodious Guile* (Yale University Press, 1988). He has received the Bollingen Prize, the Levinson Prize and, most recently, a MacArthur Fellowship. He lives in Woodbridge, Connecticut, and is A. Bartlettt Giamatti Professor of English at Yale.

Hollander writes: " 'Days of Autumn' is part of a sequence of 144 quatrains in the *aaba* form given us by Edward Fitzgerald in his translation of Omar Khayyam's *Rubaiyat* (or 'quatrains'). It is one of a number of seasonally—rather than thematically—arranged subsequences that I have published in the last two years. Shaping a poem out of part of such a group is a little like having a box of intricately colored and shaped beads that one has made at different times and stringing a particular necklace or bracelet out of them, the beads eventually returning to the box, finally to be rearranged on an ultimate strand. A few glosses might be of interest: in (1), the name of the biblical Deborah, the prophetess, means 'bee' in Hebrew; in (5), '*moi*' is not a misprint of, but rather a pun on, '*mois*'; in (6), a familiar song stanza lies encrypted in the quatrain; in (7), Paul Celan's words mean 'Is it summer? Summer *was*.' 'Epipromethean' in (18) is my coinage, of course; it combines the visions of the Titans, the foresight of Prometheus and the hindsight of Epimetheus; I have always been fascinated by the antithetical temporal and spatial sense of our English 'before.' "

RICHARD HOWARD was born in Cleveland in 1929. He is University Professor of English at Houston University, and is at work on a new translation of Marcel Proust's novel *In Search of Lost Time*. His tenth book of poems will be published by Cornelia and Michael Bessie (Random House) in 1992.

Of "Like Most Revelations," Howard writes: "The paintings of Morris Louis were created, for the most part, by tilting the canvas so that the paint could slide across the surface, staining it according to the artist's determination. The poem attempts to respond to the exigencies of this novel fashion of producing an image."

LYNDA HULL was born in Newark, New Jersey, in 1954, and has traveled widely. At present, she lives in Chicago and teaches in the M.F.A. program at Vermont College. Her poetry has won her a fellowship from the National Endowment for the Arts. Her first collection, *Ghost Money*, was published in 1986 by the University of Massachusetts Press as that year's Juniper Prize selection. *Star Ledger*, her second book, was chosen as an Edwin Ford Piper Prize winner and appeared in 1991 from the University of Iowa Press.

Hull writes: " 'Lost Fugue for Chet' grew out of an obsession with Baker's music and the eerie conjunction of a stay in Amsterdam that coincided with his final concert and death under ambiguous circumstances. About a year later I found myself saturating hours with his music, especially that last music when his voice is so ravaged, so fissured, so much more complex than the younger voice. The inwardness of the music, the way Baker's phrasing admits enough silence to build worlds, a whole drifting city in its various tempers haunted me and grew within, the way elegy so often does, fusing with memory. And then his life too: the fact that, despite a decade-long narcotics' addiction and all the pain that it spelled, all the teasing of death conscious or not, he wrought music of such piercing beauty, compelled me so much that I had to try to speak to that experience."

LAWRENCE JOSEPH was born in Detroit, Michigan, in 1948. He is a professor of law at St. John's University School of Law. Educated at the University of Michigan, where he received the Hopwood Award for Poetry, at Cambridge University, where he read English Literature, and at the University of Michigan Law School, he has published two books of poems, *Shouting at No One* (1983) and *Curriculum Vitae* (1988), both from the University of Pittsburgh Press. He has received a National Endowment for the Arts fellowship in poetry. His work was included in the 1989 edition of *Best American Poetry*. He lives in New York City.

Joseph writes: "In 'Some Sort of Chronicler I Am,' I probe the 'poetic space' that exists between 'the pressure of the contemporaneous' and 'the poetry of the contemporaneous,' Wallace Stevens's terms in 'The Irrational Element in Poetry' (written during the Great Depression). Within the poem, reality is both set apart, and combined with, the poem's own sense of what the poetry of reality is. The poem employs different tones of voice to get to the heart of the matter. The couplet form—with its in-between spaces—allows the voices to switch between the realities depicted in the poem to an awareness of the act of making a poem about them. My poetry, from the very beginning, has explored the connections between reality and the poetry that creates and recreates it. 'Some Sort of Chronicler I Am' is an *ars poetica*. It is a poem about poetry, a poem aware of itself as poetry, expressing the pressure of reality."

GALWAY KINNELL was born in Providence, Rhode Island, in 1927. He is the author of ten collections of poems, including *Selected Poems*, for which he was awarded both the Pulitzer Prize and the American Book Award, and, most recently, *When One Has Lived a Long Time Alone* (Knopf, 1990). His other awards include the Poetry Society of America's Shelley Memorial Award, the Award of Merit Medal for poetry from the American Academy of Arts and Letters, and a MacArthur Foundation fellowship. Mr. Kinnell has also translated several collections of poems from the French. He is Samuel F. B. Morse Professor in the Faculty of Arts and Sciences at New York University, where he teaches in the graduate creative writing program.

CAROLYN KIZER was born in Spokane, Washington, in 1925. She has published seven books of poems including *Yin* (BOA Editions) which won the Pulitzer Prize in 1985. She lives most of the time in Sonoma and part of the time in Paris with her husband, John M. Woodbridge, an architect and planner. A book of her essays and criticism called *pRoses* will appear in 1992 from Copper Canyon Press.

Of "Twelve O'Clock," Kizer writes: "The inspiration for this poem came from an article in the *San Francisco Chronicle* about the widow of the late E. O. Lawrence, with a photograph of a very beautiful old lady. Mary Lawrence was trying to have her husband's name left off the Lawrence-Livermore lab, where some of the most horrendous experiments with 'nuclear devices' are carried out. She felt that this was a desecration of his name and his philosophy. The University of California said that it was not in a legal position to make the change and bucked the whole thing to the U.S. Senate. I wrote to Senator Alan Cranston. No reply. He was evidently too preoccupied with the affairs of Charles Keating. Nothing happened. But Mrs. Lawrence had become a muse of mine. I, who had never taken anything beyond a general science course in high school, began to study books on physics. It was comforting, in a way, to learn that a great many unused little gray cells were still capable of functioning in the brain of this aging person. I kept reading in physics for about two years—not scientific tomes but popular accounts.

"At the same time I had begun the poem. There were a number of things I wanted to accomplish in the poem that gave me great pleasure as I rearranged and revised. First, the dialectic of the poem: Einstein's and my mother's belief in an essentially orderly universe, versus Heisenberg's and my belief in a universe that is random and disorderly. Second, I wanted the action of the poem to reflect the Einsteinian concept of simultaneity: everything happens at once! This resulted in hours of paper shuffling and line rearranging. The stanzas were cut up and lying on the floor while I bent over them in stocking feet and pushed them around. Third, I wanted the poem to be a piece of autobiography, to include everything—pathetically little!—that I had ever thought or heard about atomic physics and the use of the atom bomb. The question I am most often asked about the poem is whether the events described 'really happened.' Quite unreasonably, for someone who believes in personal privacy and the maintenance of the idea of the *persona*, this always makes me indignant. Of course it happened just as I say it did, including the dialogue. I have a spotty memory for many things, but I remember conversations word for word, including Mother's 'Listen, darling . . .' when I was four.

"Obviously, it was a long time between conception and publication. I agree with Pope that one should take one's time about printing a poem; I also concur in his belief that revision, if one keeps at it, can be as creative and exciting as the initial act of composition. Neither of these notions have much credence today among some younger poets; it's possible that some of them don't know what they're missing."

PHYLLIS KOESTENBAUM was born in Brooklyn, New York, in 1930. She graduated from Radcliffe College. She has received grants from the National Endowment for the Arts, the Santa Clara County Arts Council, and the Money for Women/Barbara Deming Memorial Fund, and has been in residence at the MacDowell Colony and the Djerassi Foundation. Her books include *oh I can't she says* (Christopher's Books, 1980) and *That Nakedness* (Jungle Garden Press, 1982). She has recently completed two sonnet manuscripts, *Criminal Sonnets* and *Scene of the Crime*. She teaches at West Valley College in Saratoga, California, and is an affiliated scholar at Stanford University's Institute for Research on Women and Gender.

Of "Admission of Failure," Koestenbaum writes: "The poem, like many of mine, came to completion slowly. I wanted to describe an ordinary dinner that, like everything ordinary, was not in the least commonplace, that took place at a moment, like every moment in my life, pivotal. As usual, with people to stare at, I imagined their lives, this time imagining myself, sketchily, not having someone else's life, but as someone else, in someone else's life, and with that someone in mine. All that I consciously imagined is in the poem. Writing the scene, obsessed by it, I did not know what part to put in and what part to leave out, and for a long time I did not know if it belonged in lines or in a prose paragraph. In some way, this decision was the hardest. Of course, all that squirming was linked to what the poem, the paragraph, is clearly about, or so I think."

SHARON KRINSKY was born in New York City in 1945 and currently lives in the East Village. She works as a copy editor and is a graduate student in library and information science at Pratt Institute. Her poetry has appeared in *Renegade, Beet, Paragraph, Brooklyn Review* and other publications. She definitely plans to have a book of poetry out before the millennium.

Of "Mystery Stories," Krinsky writes: "I was in a poetry workshop at the 63rd Street Y and had an assignment to write a poem in parts. Reading through my old journals for inspiration, I was drawn to the dreams. They had imagery, detail, intrigue, and they posed enigmatic questions. In one dream, Allen Ginsberg said: 'Suppose you feed a baby and after chewing its food, the baby spits it all out. Whose fault is it?' When I started writing the mystery stories I stumbled on a form I had been thinking about for a long time. I was looking for a way to combine a natural, deadpan kind of voice with a spare style. I did a lot of eliminating, in the end putting what I considered essential back in to each ministory."

MAXINE KUMIN was born in Philadelphia in 1925, holds a B.A. and M.A. from Radcliffe College, and now lives on a farm in New Hampshire where she and her husband raise horses. She has taught at a number of universities, including Brandeis, Columbia, MIT and Princeton, and has been a Woodrow Wilson Fellow in Montana, Maryland, and North Carolina. Her tenth collection of poems, *Looking for Luck*, was published by W. W. Norton in 1992. Her fourth book, *Up Country*, won the Pulitzer Prize for poetry in 1973. Kumin has also published four novels, a collection of short stories, two collections of essays, and a number of children's books.

Of "Saga: Four Variations on the Sonnet," Kumin writes: "The notion of writing a group of sonnets that are thematically linked suggested itself while I was grappling with the first of these. It is always a challenge to work in a tight form and when it goes well, I think of it as a pleasure. Form in its own paradoxical way is a liberator, enabling the poet to confront hard truths within its constraints. I felt that the form gave me permission here to deal with material I might not otherwise have been driven to confront."

EVELYN LAU was born in Vancouver, Canada, in 1971. She is the author of an autobiography, *Runaway: Diary of a Street Kid* (HarperCollins, 1989) and two collections of poetry, *You Are Not Who You Claim* (Press Porcepic, 1990) and *Oedipal Dreams* (Beach Holme, 1992). *Runaway* was a Canadian best-seller, has been translated into four languages, and is being filmed as a CBC television movie. She lives in Vancouver and is working on a prose collection on sex and sadomasochism.

Lau writes: " 'Green' was written as part of a series of poems about therapy. I was nineteen and ready to leave the psychiatrist I had been seeing for four years. He had once talked about the emergence of the leaves in spring and how he was never able to capture the exact moment before they came out entirely—the moment when they were just shadows in the trees, the faintest trace of color among the branches. This seemed to me a lot like poetry—that struggle to capture a moment on paper, to keep it and hold on to it before it changes into something else. I think 'Green' expressed the wistfulness I felt at termination, and the awareness that we would continue in our separate professions to try to nail down the equivalent of that moment between the bare branches and the beginning of another season."

LI-YOUNG LEE was born in Jakarta, Indonesia, in 1957. Currently unemployed, he lives in Chicago with his wife and two children. He has received grants from the National Endowment for the Arts, the Guggenheim Foundation, and the Whiting Foundation. His first book, *Rose* (1986), won the Delmore Schwartz Memorial Poetry Award, and his second book, *The City in Which I Love You* (1990), was the Lamont Poetry Selection for 1990. Both books were published by BOA Editions Limited.

Of "This Hour and What Is Dead," Lee writes: "Looking at the poem now, a few years after it was made, I see it moves from one feeling to another; from tenderness for the personal (a dead brother, a dead father) to disaffection for the impersonal (an impersonal God). What begins as a love poem for the passed away ends as a quarrel with the eternal."

DIONISIO D. MARTÍNEZ was born in Cuba in 1956. He has lived in exile since 1965. A resident of Tampa, Florida, since 1972, he works in the Poets in the Schools program there and is public relations consultant for *Organica Quarterly*. His book *History as a Second Language* (Ohio State University Press) was published in 1992, as was *Dancing at the Chelsea*, which won the 1991 State Street Press Chapbook Competition. His work has appeared in *Michigan Quarterly Review* and *Virginia Quarterly Review* as well as in *Iowa Review*.

Of "Across These Landscapes of Early Darkness," Martínez writes: "It was 1982–83. We were listening to The Talking Heads, The Clash, Ultravox, Derribos Arias, Décima Víctima, Parálisis Permanente, Jim Carroll, Patti Smith—whatever made us believe that we looked like perfect dancers. We believed in elegance and little else. I lived in northern Spain. The presidential elections made us dance a little faster. It's easy to dance when death is tugging at your sleeves. Each day the papers brought new violence: bombings, mostly. On the eve of the election, the Spanish secret service uncovered elaborate plans for a coup d'état against someone not yet in power. Fortunately, the right people stepped in at the right time. The elections went on as scheduled. The killings, unfortunately, continued as well. But once the ballots were cast, a collective sigh was heard throughout the peninsula. We kept dancing, and drinking *sidra*, and wearing our fashionably correct smiles. It was my cousin Javier's first year as a voting citizen. We attended every fringe political rally—for the music, not the ideology: the more extremist the party, the better the music. Middle-of-the-road bands tended to play the more conservative rallies. When I returned to the States, I discovered a song called 'The Politics of Dancing.' It meant so much more after that year in Europe, after the bomb that barely missed me on my way to France. In early '83 I ran out of money and came home to a different kind of dancing. Elegance as we'd defined it was being replaced very slowly by a kind of dullness, like leather too long under the sun. Our smiles, we learned the hard way, had also become victims of the elements. That year, after a long silence, I wrote very seriously. Javier went into the army. Neither one of us had a choice. In the States, my father died as a result of a car accident. Shortly thereafter, Javier's father died a similar death on a Spanish road. Years later, in a letter, Javier said he was turning more and more into his father. He confessed not only liking the feeling, but being proud of it. I too was noticing in myself an increasingly strong resemblance to my father—or so I liked to think. My father's mannerisms, maybe a trace of his voice or just a tendency to balance my checkbook very meticulously . . . Toward the end of the decade, the world was very different: Western Europe and Javier had grown up and accepted North America for what it was, for what it still is. When a poem is about the lessons of grief, it takes a long time to surface. Patience, patience. I am looking for a new song that dances on itself, out of time. So often, we know exactly what we want. Patience is also a kind of elegance."

MEKEEL MCBRIDE was born in Pittsburgh in 1950. She currently lives in Dover, New Hampshire, and is an associate professor of English at the University of New Hampshire. Her books include *Red Letter Days* (1988), *The Going Under of the Evening Land* (1983), and *No Ordinary World* (1979), all from Carnegie Mellon University Press. She has received two grants from the National Endowment for the

Arts and is currently putting together a new book of poems called *The Tree of Life*.

Of "All Hallows' Eve," McBride writes: "A friend and I are talking about how terrifying Halloween really is. You put on a costume and suddenly you've taken your interior and made it visible. My friend locks the door, turns out the lights, and hides in the back of the house, because he can't stand all the demons coming to his door. I keep getting a picture of this kid running down a road all wrapped up in a filthy sheet. She's supposed to be a ghost. But the costume turns out to be real and it isn't, after all, Halloween. This poem, originally four times as long as it is now, shows up in my journal for about a year in various versions. It takes me that long to figure out who is running away and why. It also takes that long to pare it down to what is essential."

JAMES MCCORKLE was born in St. Petersburg, Florida, in 1954. He took his graduate degree from the University of Iowa. He is the author of *The Still Performance: Writing, Self, and Interconnection in Five Postmodern American Poets* (University of Virginia Press, 1989) and the editor of *Conversant Essays: Contemporary Poets in Poetry* (Wayne State University Press, 1990). His work was included in the 1989 edition of *The Best American Poetry*. In 1990, he received an Ingram Merrill fellowship. He currently teaches at Hobart and William Smith Colleges in Geneva, New York.

McCorkle writes: "The enigma of cities seems in retrospect my concern in " '. . . The Storm is Passing Over'; She Sang." The poem is an overlay of places, the grounding being Giorgione's *Tempesta*. Giorgione depicts a city besieged by a violent storm while in the foreground a man with a staff gazes across a stream toward a woman nursing a child. She has turned her eyes from the man to us and beyond, implicating us in the painting's immediate drama, history and future. Aside from the truly ominous storm, all remains enigmatic, including the inconclusive but disturbing iconography. The city, though sunlit while the storm begins to roll over it, is empty and silent, as though cloistered from the plague that killed Giorgione in 1510. The poem, however, did not begin with the painting, but with a snowy, upstate day, which precipitated thoughts of New York City, where I had worked for several years. Thinking of the architectures of cities caught in storms metaphorical and literal, I found myself turning to Giorgione. The phrase, 'The Storm is Passing Over,' is from a gospel song heard on the radio."

JERRY MCGUIRE was born in 1947 on January 19 (Janice Joplin, Robert E. Lee, Edgar A. Poe) in Stuyvesant Falls, New York. He has occupied himself in the air force, factories (papermaking and jet aircraft), and more universities than Charles Foster Kane is said to have attended. He holds academic degrees from Middlesex Community College, Wesleyan University, and SUNY Buffalo, and is presently managing editor of *College Literature* at West Chester University in West Chester, Pennsylvania, where he also teaches part-time. His book of poems, *The Flagpole Dance*, was published in 1990 by Lynx House Press. He calls his new manuscript *Vulgar Exhibitions*.

Of "Terminal," McGuire writes: "Poetic language can rock and roll, and does, unreasonably. Or it can jangle like a charm bracelet, and that's all right, too: for it is *just* like jewelry when it is making that noise, it is doing the intricate work of untellable displacements, strategies of a ferocious, buck-passing distraction from fixities both inner and outer. Some of this is no doubt harmless; but by its nature and definition, none of it is innocent: the racket of poetic language is always motivated, a desperate lunging of crossing lines of forced detachment and attachment.

"And we say sometimes of some prose, that there is 'poetry beneath it.' That is supposed to be a good sign—as if electrical signals from the brain of a corpse weren't merely terrifying. That passionate reeling can sometimes be felt through the steady walk of the thing simply said.

"Rarely do we think well of the reverse of this. We would *hate* to say, *beneath this poem's skin beats a heart of prose.* But 'Terminal'—whose 'experience' must come from the two years I spent crossing East European borders, and the other years I've spent numb-struck at the myriad lines drawn in the quotidian sand of American life—feels to me a poem unusually stripped of its noise, as if this once I had worked my way not *up* to a poem or *over there* to something like prose statement but somehow *out of it all* to a very cold place in me that required an extreme quiet to speak.

"And yet I can honestly say that reduced to or liberated into this space I do not know whether the end of the poem alludes to Kafka, or merely pretends to do so. One is so far from oneself."

SANDRA MCPHERSON was born in San Jose, California, in 1943. She teaches at the University of California at Davis, where she lives. The University of Illinois Press will publish her sixth collection, *The God of Indeterminacy*, in 1993. Previous books are *Streamers* (Ecco, 1988), *Patron Happiness* (Ecco, 1983), *The Year of Our Birth* (Ecco, 1978), *Radiation* (Ecco, 1973), and *Elegies for the Hot Season* (Indiana University Press, 1970).

Of "Choosing an Author for Assurance in the Night," McPherson writes: "Waking at 3 A.M. one night, I tried to read to fend off a barrage of discouraging thoughts. But the writer I chose talked too much, with a constant flurry of virtuosic effects. On an earlier poem, 'Women and Vision,' I had displaced my own anxiety by 'taking dictation' from a Mexican Day of the Dead figure, a skeletal writer at her typewriter. I turned to her again—and found her perspective healthy and corrective. She was not showing off. And she liked herself—as is. I look forward to further advice from her; she is a writer I can learn from."

ROBERT MORGAN was born in Hendersonville, North Carolina, in 1944. He teaches at Cornell University and lives in Freeville, New York. He received a Guggenheim Fellowship in 1988, and the James G. Hanes Poetry Prize from the Fellowship of Southern Writers in 1991. Among his nine books of poetry are *Red Owl* (W. W. Norton, 1972); *Sigodlin* (Wesleyan University Press, 1990); and *Green River: New and Selected Poems* (Wesleyan University Press, 1991). A book of stories, *The Blue Valleys*, was brought out in 1989 by Peachtree Publishers, which will issue *The Mountains Won't Remember Us and Other Stories* in 1992.

Morgan writes: "When I began writing 'Honey' I was thinking only of the culture of beekeeping. I remembered that not only were knowledge and skill involved, but for the best results, courtesy was also important. To work with bees you have to try to see things from their point of view, to understand and respect their protocol. Only by consideration of their needs and fears can the gift of honey be taken. But as I approached the end of the poem it occurred to me that the compact richness of honey was much like that of poetry. I saw the crystal permanence of the honey as a figure for the sprawling vernacular quickness of speech gathered to essential, timeless latin in poetry."

THYLIAS MOSS was born in Cleveland in 1954. She teaches at Phillips Academy in Andover, Massachusetts. *Pyramid of Bone* (University of Virginia Press, 1989), her second book of poems, was nominated for the National Book Critics Circle Award. She has since published two new collections: *At Redbones* (Cleveland State University Press, 1990) and *Rainbor Remnants in Rock Bottom Ghetto Sky*, which Charles Simic selected for the National Poetry Series (Persea Books, 1991). She has received a poetry fellowship from the National Endowment for the Arts. Her work was included in the 1989, 1990, and 1991 editions of *The Best American Poetry*.

Moss writes: " 'An Anointing' is all in italics just as it should be, I think, in order to consecrate the moment in which these two girls, Molly and the speaker, simultaneously become aware of personal holiness, of the sacredness just of existence. What is wondrous is the simultaneity; both girls arrive at identical knowledge with the exact timing that permits sharing and therefore communion. It is a poem of unity where unity may also mean acquisition of self-wholeness, sort of like the reintegration of multiple personalities into one. Each learns to be her own salvation, and the poem is a celebration of that learning. One praises, elevates the other at the same time. It is a poem of exemplary self-esteem and of both personal and community triumph. The poem emphasizes the logic of discovery and insists upon honest exploration of identity. Accordingly, the poem is also about acceptance. Molly and the speaker quite simply are best friends, two adolescent girls who recognize the potential of their relationship to be their only legitimate claim to true love. These are such empowering, such liberating ideas and sentiments that the occasion of the poem is immortalized. No matter what occurs in their lives, this moment will always be for them just as it was, as it is. As for the lesbian implications of the poem, well, they are absolutely necessary, fundamental to the girls' discovery. Whether or not their lives are eventually heterosexually realized, they need first to come to terms with their femaleness in ways conducive to triumph, respect, integrity, and joy. They discover what is wonderful and worthy, perhaps even superior, in being female, so are therefore most able to encourage and praise each other. All needs are met. They are girls without deficits. They are so whole and so aware of their vitality that they know they qualify as goddesses. And just as supernatural beings have to do, Molly and the speaker give birth to each other. They do whatever they have to do. With such ability, how can they ever be without what they need? So, yes; they're a bit smug, but nevertheless they are enviable.

"Is Molly real? Indeed she is within the context of the poem, but this Molly is not based on anything but my own feeling of completion. If these girls had to be derived from reality, then I would say that they are two parts of myself embracing and coming together; me getting acquainted with me as only I can. Beyond that, the poem is an attempt to recapture the best and mischievous part of youth, a real exercise in curiosity and approval."

CAROL MUSKE was born in St. Paul, Minnesota, in December 1945. She is a professor in the English department at the University of Southern California, where she teaches creative writing. Her fifth book of poems, entitled *Red Trousseau*, and her second novel, *Saving St. Germ*, will be published in 1993 by Viking Penguin. She has been the recipient of fellowships from the Guggenheim and Ingram Merrill foundations. Her other books of poetry are *Camouflage* (University of Pittsburgh Press, 1975), *Skylight* (Doubleday, 1981), *Wyndmere* (University of Pittsburgh Press, 1985), and *Applause* (University of Pittsburgh Press, 1989). She is also the author of the novel *Dear Digby* (Viking Penguin, 1989), which is being made into a feature film.

Muske writes: " 'Red Trousseau' connects and interweaves two 'meditations.' The first is a contemporary woman's reflection on the nature of desire (her own) and the second meditation is an historical and feminist take on the image of a woman burning: a symbol of both the annihilation of the independent feminine (the witch trials and executions) and the seductive power of passion.

"Because it scared me to write this poem and because the poem continues to disturb me, I find I don't have a lot to say about it. Usually I manage to develop a cheerful, slightly avuncular relationship with completed, published poems—especially over time—but this one continues to resist placement around the hearthfire. Perhaps because it continues to burn in an odder, wilder place. Who knows."

MARY OLIVER lives in Provincetown, Massachusetts, but she is currently at Sweet Briar College in Virginia where she is the Margaret Banister Writer-in-Residence. Her *New and Selected Poems* will be published by Beacon Press in the fall of 1992. While at Sweet Briar College she is completing a book "primarily on the teaching of poetry, but which contains some other more personal commentary as well."

Of "Rain," Oliver writes: "After years of writing the short, intense lyric, I am curious about the longer, less-focused, more leisurely work. Instead of taking the reader by the hand and running him down the hill, I want to lead him into a house of many rooms, and leave him alone in each of them. I want the reader to feel out the connections for himself, instead of stating them pretty explicitly. Such a poem allows for wider interpretation, no doubt; also it offers greater range of expression, including the narrative as well as the more personal 'rhapsodic.'

"I don't mean to imply that such a poem-form is new—only that it is new to me."

MICHAEL PALMER was born in New York City in 1943. While at Harvard College he edited *Joglars* magazine with Clark Coolidge. He took his graduate degree in comparative literature at Harvard and moved to San Francisco in 1969. Since 1974 he has collaborated on more than a dozen dance works with the choreographer Margaret Jenkins. He has also worked with numerous composers and performance artists. His radio plays, *Idem* I–IV, were produced for KQED radio in 1980. Books and chapbooks include *Plan of the City of O* (Barn Dream Press, 1971), *Blake's Newton* (Black Sparrow Press, 1972), *C's Songs* (Sand Dollar Press, 1973), *The Circular Gates* (Black Sparrow Press, 1974), *Without Music* (Black Sparrow Press, 1977), *Transparency of the Mirror* (Little Dinosaur Press, 1980), *Alogon* (Tuumba Press, 1980), *Notes for Echo Lake* (North Point Press, 1981), *First Figure* (North Point Press, 1984) and *Sun* (North Point Press, 1988). He is the editor of *Code of Signals: Recent Writings in Poetics* (North Atlantic Books, 1983) and has translated *Jonah Who*

Will Be 25 in the Year 2000, by Alain Tanner and John Berger, for the same press. He has published a number of other translations, including most recently (with Norma Cole) *The Surrealists Look at Painting*, from Lapis Press. In the past two years he has completed collaborations with the painters Michaëla Henich and Sandro Chia. He has been awarded two National Endowment for the Arts fellowships in poetry and was a Guggenheim Fellow in poetry during 1989–90. He is a contributing editor to *Sulfur* magazine and has lectured and taught at many universities throughout the United States. A volume of selected essays, interviews, and talks is forthcoming from the University of New Mexico Press.

Palmer writes: " 'Eighth Sky' is written in memory of the French poet Max Jacob. It was begun while passing through St.-Benoît-sur-Loire, site of the monastery where Jacob, friend of Picasso, mentor of Edmond Jabès, sacred clown, homosexual, and Jew turned Catholic mystic, was arrested by the Gestapo in 1944. He died soon after of pneumonia at the Drancy transfer camp. The poem employs a number of Jacob's own phrases, particularly from *Le Cornet à dés* (*The Dice Box*)."

ROBERT PINSKY was born in the historic seaside resort town of Long Branch, New Jersey, in 1940. His books of poetry include *The Want Bone*, *History of My Heart*, and *An Explanation of America*. His most recent collection of essays is *Poetry and the World*. After several years in California, he now teaches in the graduate creative writing program of Boston University.

Of "Avenue," Pinsky writes: "Ideas get into our heads and we pursue them, sometimes for years or forever. Long ago, possibly influenced by Pound's definition of the epic as a poem containing history, I proposed to myself that poetry must imagine a community. That the emphasis needed to be on *imagine* I could tell from reading my first hero in the art, Yeats. (What if I had attached myself to Stevens, instead?)

"So my poem 'Avenue' is one foray in a lifelong quest among the pronouns, *they*, *I*, *we*, *he*, *her* and underneath them their provisional or arbitrary quality. Shall we tell it to you in the first person? Would you tell it to them in the third person? Might I try it in the second person? And so forth.

"The poem also has roots in the High Holy Days as I experienced them as a child—the hypnotic appeal in fasting; the boredom and sudden emotion of the prayers; pitching horse chestnuts against the back wall of the synagogue; people in stylish or frumpy dress-up clothes; the foreign otherworldly sensuousness of cantorial singing; the climactic yet anticlimactic groan of the ram's horn; my grandparents on one side watching Perry Como sing the *Kol Nidre* on television; my grandfather on the other side avoiding the whole scene of devotion; the secular and Christian world with its bright seductive October weather, its downtown, its Atlantic Ocean, radiating and pulling on all sides away from the synagogue at the center.

"Though little of that material figures directly in the poem, 'Avenue' is concerned with the peculiar English name of the Day of Atonement. 'Atonement,' that looks like some Latin borrowing, is made out of the idea of being 'at one' with one's god, or community, or vows, or even a person. Yom Kippur is the day of at-one-ment, which chimes interestingly for me with the Christian and pagan holiday of the same time of year: All Saints or All Spirits. All, one: a play of unity and diversity that in turn makes me think of the fragmented, plural American city held together visibly by words, by the signs and spoken or sung syllables of its streets, where all our 'they' is also somehow 'one.'

"One fall, driving along the Finchley Road in London I saw in my headlights a man lying in the roadway. He was passed-out drunk. I carried him into the entryway of a shoe store, an incident I tell here from his point of view, in the first person, as *I*, as one of all."

LAWRENCE RAAB was born in Pittsfield, Massachusetts in 1946. He is the author of three collections of poems—*Mysteries of the Horizon* (Doubleday, 1972), *The Collector of Cold Weather* (The Ecco Press, 1976), and *Other Children* (Carnegie-Mellon, 1987). He has received the Bess Hokin Prize from *Poetry* magazine, a Junior Fellowship from the University of Michigan Society of Fellows, and grants from the Massachusetts Council on the Arts and the National Endowment for the Arts. He lives in Williamstown, Massachusetts where he teaches writing and literature at Williams College.

Of "The Sudden Appearance of a Monster at a Window," Raab writes: "The image in the poem's title is one I felt I could trust a reader to recall from any number of movies, stories, or illustrations.

The monster appears and a moment of paralysis results, full of various horrific possibilities. Yet the 'you' in my poem does not then scream or retreat in terror, as might be expected. And the monster finally just turns away. I wanted my character—whom I imagine to be a woman even though I know the poem provides no specific details—to respond in a manner that at first might seem admirably levelheaded, even brave. No shrieking or fainting. But no recognition either—no compassion, finally no real concern for this mysterious visitation. She returns quickly to the business at hand. Perhaps the monster leaves because he recognizes a certain lack of imagination in her face, because he belongs to a world too different from hers, because no interesting story would result from any further intrusion into her life. If the poem succeeds in suggesting any such possibility, then the enigmatic monster will be more than a figure of the grotesque, and my character's resolute practicality might become a kind of sad dismissal of the unknown, the otherworldly, the marvelous."

LIAM RECTOR was born in Washington, D.C., in 1949. He spent the past year studying the First Amendment and cultural policy at the Kennedy School of Government at Harvard and taught a course on censorship at Emerson College. He has published *The Sorrow of Architecture*, a book of poems (Dragon Gate, 1984), and was the editor of *The Day I Was Older: On the Poetry of Donald Hall* (Story Line, 1989). He has administered various literary programs and is currently director of the Bennington Writing Workshops at Bennington College.

Of "The Night the Lightning Bugs Lit Last in the Field Then Went Their Way," Rector writes: "Meaning in motion passes through the triadic stanza much as water passes through the green garden hose on its way to the plant—rushing, touching such solids as there are, inherently integral, nothing to do but proceed. 'I can't go on; I'll go on,' said Mr. B. The beauty of that stanzaic form got me to this poem and provided the net for its fucking meaning."

DONALD REVELL was born in New York City in 1954. He lives in Denver where he is editor of *Denver Quarterly* and an associate professor of English at Denver University. His published collections are *From the Abandoned Cities* (Harper & Row, 1983), *The Gaza of Winter* (University of Georgia Press, 1988), and *New Dark Ages* (Wesleyan, 1990).

Revell writes: " 'Plenitude' is one of a series of longer poems I have written in the attempt to emulate symphonic form in verse. The thematic purpose of the poem is to discover and to propound those fine distinctions that make an honorable private life possible; and it seemed to me that Beethoven is the composer most splendidly able to elevate fine distinctions to the level of high art, to take a very few notes and, by exploring their subtlest tonic distinctions, create a music of great moral force. 'Plenitude' is especially indebted to the Seventh Symphony, the second movement of which is a miracle of statement through variation."

ADRIENNE RICH was born in Baltimore in 1929. She is the author of many volumes of poetry, including *The Fact of a Doorframe: Poems Selected and New 1950–1984* (1984), *Time's Power* (1989), and *An Atlas of the Difficult World* (1991), all from W. W. Norton. Her three prose books are *Of Woman Born: Motherhood as Experience and Institution* (1976, revised edition 1986), *On Lies, Secrets and Silence* (1979) and *Blood, Bread and Poetry* (1986), also from Norton. She was the first recipient of the Ruth Lilly Prize for outstanding achievement in American poetry. She has received the Brandeis Creative Arts Commission Medal for Poetry, the Fund for Human Dignity Award from the National Gay Task Force, and the Common Wealth Award in literature. She is a founding editor of the Jewish feminist journal *Bridges*. She has lived in California since 1984.

Of "For a Friend in Travail," Rich writes: "The poem began, and begins, with a nightmare. Then, the attempt to imagine the night-waking, the night dread, of a friend far away and dangerously ill. The question comes from Simone Weil's *Waiting for God*: 'The love of our neighbor in all its fullness simply means being able to say to him: "What are you going through?" ' The poppy here is not a flower of sleep but the red-gold California poppies bursting from earth in late winter, a breaking-open into life. The poem embodies a tension between love for the world and desire for oblivion, between surrender and struggle, between nightmare and the sweetness of life."

LEN ROBERTS was born in Cohoes, New York, in 1947. He teaches at Northampton Community College in Bethlehem, Pennsylvania, where he lives with his wife and three children. He has received a Guggenheim Fellowship in Poetry and two National Endowment for the Arts creative writing awards. Roberts' most recent book, *Black Wings*, was selected for the National Poetry Series and was published by Persea Books in 1989. Other books of poetry include *Sweet Ones* (Milkweed Editions, 1988); *From the Dark* (State University of New York Press, 1984); and *Cohoes Theater* (Momentum Press, 1981). He has a chapbook of poems, *Learning about the Heart*, to be published by Silverfish Press in July 1992, and a volume of his translations of the selected poems of Sandor Csoori, a leading Hungarian poet, will be published by Copper Canyon Press in April, 1992.

Of "We Sat, So Patient," Roberts writes: "This poem deals with the innocent belief we somehow had when we were young that knowledge might ultimately save us. Sister Ann Zita, as an emissary of God, serves well as the black Angel of Death, even as she says it's God's will. None of us knew what was coming."

DAVID ST. JOHN was born in Fresno, California, in 1949. He is the author of four collections of poetry, *Hush* (1976), *The Shore* (1980), *No Heaven* (1985), all from Houghton Mifflin, and *Terraces of Rain* (Recursos Books, 1991), as well as three limited edition books, *The Olive Grove* (1980), *The Orange Piano* (1987), and *The Unsayable, the Unknowable, and You* (1992). He has received grants and fellowships from the John Simon Guggenheim Memorial Foundation, the National Endowment for the Arts, the Ingram Merrill Foundation, and the Maryland Arts Council. *Hush* was awarded the Great Lakes College Association Prize as the best first book of poetry of 1976; *The Shore* was awarded the James D. Phelan Prize from the San Francisco Foundation. In 1984, St. John received the Rome Fellowship in Literature, awarded by the American Academy and Institute of Arts and Letters. He is poetry editor of the *Antioch Review* and professor of English at the University of Southern California.

St. John writes: "I'd wanted for many years to write a poem with the same title as George Meredith's famous sonnet, 'Lucifer in Starlight.' I knew that I wanted the poem to be a dramatic monologue in which Lucifer spoke in a contemporary setting; I also knew the line from the Meredith sonnet that I'd use as an epigraph. Other than these rather vague beginnings, I had no idea of the shape the poem might take. In the spring of 1989, I went back to Rome, where I'd lived during the 1984–85 academic year (at the American Academy). On my drive from the airport into Rome, I recalled a conversation I'd had with a friend at a party the night before I left Los Angeles, a conversation about the relative virtues of Greece and Italy; it suddenly occurred to me that I finally knew how to begin 'Lucifer in Starlight.' The poem is a kind of love poem to Rome itself and to the luxuriant sensuality of the city.''

LYNDA SCHRAUFNAGEL was born in Ashland, Wisconsin, in 1950, and died of lymphocytomatosis in 1991. Her poems have appeared in *Shenandoah*, *Western Humanities Review*, and *The Best American Poetry 1989*.

In an elegy for Schraufnagel entitled "To the Tenth Muse: A Recommendation,'' Richard Howard, her teacher and editor, writes:

> Angular, graceful,
> her manic glee in assuming the mask of a scornful dyke
> deceived me about her age—I thought she was a *girl*!
> She was forty-one
>
> when she died, just now,
> but a coltish ease in each movement reinforced the style
> of adolescent insouciance I attributed to her grins . . .
> I would discover
>
> she had been married,
> *yes, but he was a transvestite*; she had greedily abused
> every substance in the book, *yes, but she was no reader*;
> the nuns had taught her
>
> to bear the ennui
> of almost any routine she would be faced with, *yes, but
> now she knew how eagerly she welcomed victimization.*
> No matter what chore—

bank-teller, waitress,
student-teacher, even the tedium of my assignments—
could be sucked into her secret knowledge: *women are dupes!*
They let men have them

    to avoid having
themselves . . .

"Genius alone / can afford to vex / itself as she did / without suffering injury," writes Howard. "She suffered." Howard's poem appears in the Autumn 1991 issue of *Southwest Review*.

ELIZABETH SPIRES was born in Lancaster, Ohio, in 1952 and grew up in nearby Circleville. Her books of poems are *Annonciade* (Viking Penguin, 1989), *Swan's Island* (Holt, 1985), and *Globe* (Wesleyan, 1981). Currently she lives in Baltimore where she is an adjunct associate visiting professor in the Writing Seminars at Johns Hopkins and writer-in-residence at Goucher College. Her work was included in the last three editions of *The Best American Poetry* and in the recently published anthology *New American Poets of the '90s* (Godine, 1991).

Spires writes: " 'Good Friday. Driving Westward.' takes place on a secular Good Friday but hearkens back in its imagery to Donne's great poem 'Good Friday. Riding Westward.' Although the setting of my poem—the beltway around a city, a mall—is determinedly modern, the transcendental dimension keeps breaking through in the speaker's consciousness, most noticeably in the image of the nailed hand at the poem's close. The 'sin' in the poem, if one can call it that, is the spiritual passivity of the speaker, a passivity bordering on despair (as embodied in the speaker's belief that God has withdrawn from the world). The poem is very much a 'dark day of the soul,' relentless in its outlook and providing no exit or spiritual solution. In this respect, it exists in stark contrast to Donne's poem."

RACHEL SRUBAS was born in LaGrange, Illinois, in 1964. She now lives in Chicago. At this writing, she is completing her M.A. in English and is teaching English composition, while she looks toward the possibility of a theological education. Her poems have appeared in *Naming the Daytime Moon: Stories and Poems by Chicago Women*, *Another Chicago Magazine*, and *Chicago Literary Review*. In 1987 she cofounded Chicago's Locked Out Poets, whose chapbook, *Love Me for My Lobby Alone*, was published by Going Down Press in 1990.

Srubas writes: " 'I Want to Marry You' came to me suddenly and whole in midsummer, while I was falling in love with another poet, whom I would, in fact, later marry. I remember sweating as I wrote it, aware that my lover was not the 'you' of the poem, and that the 'I' was using a voice I hadn't known was in me. But in order to comment on the poem, I have to talk about love, which, I've learned, plunges us into our darkest histories and then brings us back up still breathing, with artifacts to show for ourselves. Or maybe we stop breathing when we're down there. Yes, I think we do, and then love, like God, revives us, and lets us keep our memories. My poem is a souvenir of that salvation, and addresses salvation itself, in ways that mystify and surprise me."

RICHARD TILLINGHAST was born in Memphis, Tennessee, in 1940, and educated at Sewanee and Harvard. He is currently professor of English at the University of Michigan and lives in Ann Arbor. During 1990–91 he lived in Istanbul, Turkey, and Kinvara, County Galway, Ireland, as the recipient of a fellowship from the American Research Institute in Turkey and a travel grant from the Amy Lowell Trust. His books include *Sleep Watch* (1969), *The Knife and Other Poems* (1980), and *Our Flag Was Still There* (1984), all from Wesleyan University Press. "Anatolian Journey" will be included in a new collection of his poems to be published in the fall of 1993 by David Godine.

Tillinghast writes: "I wrote, or started writing 'Anatolian Journey' during an overnight bus trip from Istanbul to Sinop, on the Black Sea, where I was going to visit the family of some Turkish friends of mine. Travel itself being a form of poetry, most of the details in the poem are simply lifted from what they were in real life. *Hayat*, 'Life' in Turkish, really is the brand name for a bottled mineral water, though the pine trees appear on the bottle of a different brand not so felicitously named. I was studying Turkish at the time, hence the 'alien conjugations.'

"The interior dialogue in the poem—'So you think you're a fish now?' / 'It's true that time is a river.'—came to me in a dream. At the house where I was staying on the Bosphorus, a mile or two above the center of Istanbul, the mosquitoes tended to wake one up every night around 2:00 A.M., and then the first call to prayer from a nearby mosque would wake one again at about 4:30. Awakened abruptly like that, I found it easier than usual to remember my dreams."

LEWIS TURCO was born in Buffalo, New York, in 1934. He served as an enlisted man in the U.S. Navy from 1952–56; subsequently he took degrees from the universities of Connecticut and Iowa. In 1961 he was founding director of the Cleveland State University Poetry Center and, in 1968, of the S.U.N.Y. College at Oswego's Program in Writing Arts, which he continues to direct. He is the author of many volumes including *The Book of Forms: A Handbook of Poetics* (1968) and *The New Book of Forms* (1986). *Visions and Revisions of American Poetry* (1986) won the Melville Cane Award of the Poetry Society of America. His most recent volume of poetry is *The Shifting Web: New and Selected Poems* (1989). *A Family Album* (1990) and *Murmurs in the Walls* (1992) won the 1989 Silverfish Review Chapbook Competition and the 1990 Cooper House Chapbook Competition, respectively.

Turco writes: " 'Kamelopard' is the *K* poem in an alphabestiary of monsters titled *The Book of Beasts*. Although the entire series of poems has not been published in book form, some of the humanoid monsters appear in a chapbook titled *A Cage of Creatures* (1978), and several of the nonhumanoid creatures are collected in another chapbook titled *A Maze of Monsters* (1986).

" 'Kamelopard' appeared in neither of these. The major source for *The Book of Beasts* is Jorge Luis Borges' *The Book of Imaginary Beings*, though other sources were also used, in this case an anonymously authored book titled *The Beauties of the Creation; or, a New Moral System of Natural History* (Philadelphia, 1792). Archaic words have been used in the poems (in this case, the title itself and *mere*: 'A sheet of standing water; a lake, a pond'), many of them taken from Charles MacKay's *The Lost Beauties of the English Language* (1874). One can only agree with Mr. MacKay that there are many words that ought to be restored to English, and *The Book of Beasts* is a small attempt to reinstate a few of them. One hopes that the contexts in which the words appear suggest their definitions to the extent that a glossary becomes unnecessary. The inspiration for this particular poem was the last line, taken from an article somewhere, which is purportedly a scientific fact."

CHASE TWICHELL was born in New Haven, Connecticut, in 1950. She has published three books of poems: *Perdido* (Farrar, Straus & Giroux, 1991), *The Odds* (Pittsburgh, 1986), and *Northern Spy* (Pittsburgh, 1981). She is the coeditor of *The Practice of Poetry: Writing Exercises from Poets Who Teach* (HarperCollins, 1992). She has received grants from the National Endowment for the Arts, the Artists Foundation, and the John Simon Guggenheim Memorial Foundation. She lives in the Adirondacks and in Princeton, New Jersey, where she teaches at Princeton University.

Of "Word Silence," Twichell writes: "This poem came to me backwards. The first couple of lines arrived intact, and resisted all my efforts to make them less didactic. Normally, I'm suspicious of any phrasings that seem too conclusory, especially if a poem is still rough, since there's little excitement in writing up to a point that's a given. I was saved by the fact that the bossy lines also wanted to *open* the poem. That meant I had to start at what initially seemed a stopping point. In other words, I had to start the poem off balance, which was interesting. Furthermore, it was clearly, overtly about something that has always fascinated me: the way, when a poem is finished, its surface closes over and it dispossesses its writer, becoming alien and independent. That's why the process strikes me as sexual in its mechanism: there's a drive that can be called desire, and the desire is, in the end, to exhaust itself. To pleasure itself in articulation but also to get to the end, which is a withdrawal back into silence. I wanted to make the poem enact its own knowledge, which is why it ends in wordlessness and ignorance of itself."

ROSANNA WARREN was born in Connecticut in 1953. At present she teaches comparative literature at Boston University, and is a contributing editor of *Partisan Review*. She is the author of *Each Leaf Shines Separate* (Norton, 1984), and she edited and contributed to *The Art of Translation: Voices from the Field* (Northeastern University Press, 1989).

Of "Necrophiliac," Warren writes: "As the plangencies accumulated in my new manuscript of poems, I became suspicious of my own elegiac impulse. The Shakespearean sonnet (deformed here) came to hand, unpremeditated, as a shape into which rage, love, and writerly anxiety were accustomed to being compressed. 'Collaborate' is meant, of course, to spread its stain throughout the poem."

IOANNA-VERONIKA WARWICK was born in Poland and came to the United States when she was seventeen. Her poems have appeared in, and won prizes from, *New Letters*, *Quarterly West*, and *Sow's Ear* magazines. Her translations of Polish poetry have been published in *American Poetry Review* and *Wisconsin Review*. She holds a B.A. from UCLA and an M.F.A. from San Diego State University. She lives in California.

Of "Eyeglasses," Warwick writes: "My maternal grandparents were taken to Auschwitz in late August 1944, toward the end of the Warsaw Uprising, together with thousands of other inhabitants of suburban sections of Warsaw. My grandmother was sixty-seven, my grandfather seventy-two. The story of their survival is the subject of another poem.

"On January 18, 1945, the Nazis, in their retreat before the advancing Red Army, evacuated the camp, taking the inmates on a death march to other camps in Germany; the sick and the old, however, were allowed to stay. My grandparents stayed on for a while, with Grandmother foraging for left-behind potatoes and turnips. Then they decided to try to return to their hometown near Lodz. They walked for several days until they managed to get on a train.

"The 'small handcart' mentioned in the last line was one of the many abandoned small carts that had been used to distribute food rations.

"I deliberately left out gruesome details such as dead bodies lying on the frozen ground, eyed by crows and ravens, and chose to evoke the horror of Auschwitz through the central image of the mountain of eyeglasses."

C. K. WILLIAMS was born in Newark, New Jersey, in 1936. He is currently living in Paris, and teaches part of each year at George

Mason University, in Fairfax, Virginia. His most recent book is *A Dream of Mind*, which was published by Farrar, Straus & Giroux in May 1992.

Williams writes: " 'The Knot' is a part of the sequence that is the title poem of my new book. The poems use the conceit of dream as a way of investigating various elements of mind and consciousness. 'The Knot' deals with the way the individual mind evolves in its conceptions, and moves toward 'ideal' notions of conditions of consciousness and existence."

CHARLES WRIGHT was born in Pickwick Dam, Tennessee, in 1935. He lives in Charlottesville, Virginia, and teaches in the English department of the University of Virginia. His most recent book of poems is *The World of the Ten Thousand Things: Poems 1980–1990* (Farrar, Straus & Giroux, 1990). He was corecipient in 1983 of the National Book Award in poetry for *Country Music/Selected Early Poems* (Wesleyan University Press), a second edition of which was published in 1991. In 1988 he published *Halflife* (University of Michigan Press), a book of prose improvisations and interviews, as well as *Zone Journals* (Farrar, Straus & Giroux), a book of poems.

Wright writes: " 'Winter-Worship' is from the fourth section of a new manuscript I am working on that has the working title of *Chickamauga*. All the poems in this section so far have a suppressed first-person narration and are structurally elliptical. Structural formations and transformations are of continuing interest for me, and *Chickamauga* is a field for that interest."

FRANZ WRIGHT was born in Vienna in 1953. He has been a writing fellow at the Provincetown Fine Arts Work Center, and for a number of years taught creative writing and literature classes at Emerson College in Boston, where he continues to live. He is a current recipient of a Whiting Foundation Award, and a recent recipient of writing fellowships from the National Endowment for the Arts and the Guggenheim Foundation. His most recent full-length collections of poetry are *Entry in an Unknown Hand* (1990) and *The Night World & the Word Night* (1992), from Carnegie Mellon.

Of "Depiction of Childhood," Wright writes: "Picasso did a series of etchings of a Minotaur, in one of which you see a little girl. You expect her to be terrorized but she isn't; she's guiding him. The little girl is a symbol, though of what I'm not sure—perhaps the power of childhood, of innocence, and of the powerless."

STEPHEN YENSER was born in Wichita, Kansas, in 1941. He has lived and taught in Iraq, France, and Greece, and he is now professor of English and vice chair for graduate studies at UCLA. The recipient of an Ingram Merrill Foundation grant, two Fulbrights, and the Harvey L. Eby Award for the Art of Teaching, he has written two critical books—*Circle to Circle: The Poetry of Robert Lowell* (University of California Press, 1975) and *The Consuming Myth: The Work of James Merrill* (Harvard University Press, 1987). He has just completed his first volume of poems.

Yenser writes: " 'Vertumnal,' an elegy for my former father-in-law, evokes Vertumnus—the shape-shifting god associated with harvest, seasonal change, and (as Sir William Smith says) other occurrences in connection with which the verb *verto* is commonly used—especially as he appears in Propertius's *Elegies* (IV.2) and Ovid's *Metamorphoses* (XIV). Almost inevitably the poem draws on other works as well, from Marvell's 'garden' poems through Arnold's 'Thyrsis,' Whitman's 'Song of Myself' and Cavafy's 'Soma, thymisou' ('Body, remember'), to Raymond Bomba's own writings."

MAGAZINES WHERE THE POEMS
WERE FIRST PUBLISHED

Agni Review, ed. Askold Melnyczuk. Creative Writing Program, Boston University. 236 Bay State Road, Boston, Mass. 02215.

American Poetry Review, eds. Stephen Berg, David Bonanno, and Arthur Vogelsang. 1721 Walnut Street, Philadelphia, Pa. 19103.

Another Chicago Magazine, eds. Lee Webster and Barry Silesky. Box 11223, Chicago, Ill. 60611.

Antaeus, ed. Daniel Halpern. The Ecco Press, 100 W. Broad St., Hopewell, N.J. 08525.

The Atlantic Monthly, poetry ed. Peter Davison. 745 Boylston Street, Boston, Mass. 02116.

Boulevard, ed. Richard Burgin. 2400 Chestnut Street, #3301, Philadelphia, Pa. 19103.

The Boston Phoenix, poetry ed. Lloyd Schwartz. 126 Brookline Ave., Boston, Mass. 02215.

Brooklyn Review, eds. Michael K. Franklin and Barbara Weisberg. Brooklyn College, English Department, Brooklyn, N.Y. 11210.

Callalloo, ed. Charles H. Rowell. University of Virginia, Department of English, Wilson Hall, Charlottesville, Va. 22903.

Denver Quarterly, ed. Donald Revell. University of Denver, Colo. 80208.

Epoch, ed. Michael Koch. Cornell University, 251 Goldwin Smith Hall, Ithaca, N.Y. 14853.

Exquisite Corpse, ed. Andrei Codrescu. Culture Shock Foundation, English Department, Louisiana State University, Baton Rouge, La. 70803.

Field, eds. Stuart Friebert and David Young. Rice Hall, Oberlin College, Oberlin, Ohio 44074.

Fine Madness, eds. Sean Bentley, Louis Bergsagel, Christine Deavel, John Malek, and John Marshall. P.O. Box 31138, Seattle, Wash. 98103.

The Formalist, ed. William Baer. 525 S. Rotherwood Ave., Evansville, Ind. 47714.

The Georgia Review, ed. Stanley Lindberg. University of Georgia, Athens, Ga. 30602.

Grand Street, ed. Jean Stein. 135 Central Park West, New York, N.Y. 10023.

Hambone, ed. Nathaniel Mackey. 134 Hunolt Street, Santa Cruz, Calif. 95060.

The Iowa Review, ed. David Hamilton. 308 EPB, University of Iowa, Iowa City, Iowa 52242.

The Kenyon Review, ed. Marilyn Hacker. Kenyon College, Gambier, Ohio 43022.

Michigan Quarterly Review, ed. Laurence Goldstein. University of Michigan, 3032 Rackham Building, Ann Arbor, Mich. 48109–1070.

The New Criterion, poetry ed. Robert Richman. 850 Seventh Avenue, New York, N.Y. 10019.

New England Review, ed. T. R. Hummer. Middlebury College, Middlebury, Vt. 05753.

New Letters, ed. James McKinley. 109 Scofield Hall, University of Missouri/Kansas City, 5100 Rockhill Road, Kansas City, Mo. 64110.

The New Yorker, poetry ed. Alice Quinn. 20 West 43rd Street, New York, N.Y. 10036.

North American Review, poetry ed. Peter Cooley. University of Northern Iowa, 1227 West 27th Street, Cedar Falls, Iowa 50614

The Ohio Review, ed. Wayne Dodd. Ohio University, 320 Ellis Hall, Athens, Ohio 45701–2979.

The Paris Review, poetry ed. Patricia Storace. 541 East 72nd Street, New York, N.Y. 10021.

Ploughshares, associate poetry ed. Joyce Peseroff; rotating guest editors (for 1991, DeWitt Henry, Joyce Peseroff, and Gerald Stern). Emerson College, 100 Beacon Street, Boston, Mass. 02116.

Poetry, ed. Joseph Parisi. 60 West Walton Street, Chicago, Ill. 60610.

Raritan, ed. Richard Poirier; managing ed. Suzanne K. Hyman. Rutgers University, 31 Mine Street, New Brunswick, N.J. 08903.

The Sewanee Review, ed. George Core. University of the South, Sewanee, Tenn. 37375.

Tikkun, ed. Michael Lerner; poetry ed. for 1991, Robert Pinsky. 5100 Leona St., Oakland, Calif. 94619.

Verse, American ed. Henry Hart; guest editor for 1991, Susan M. Schultz. Department of English, College of William and Mary, Williamsburg, Va. 23185.

Western Humanities Review, poetry ed. Richard Howard. 341 Orson Spenser Hall, University of Utah, Salt Lake City, Utah 84112.

Witness, ed. Peter Stine. 31000 Northwestern Highway, Suite 200, Farmington Hills, Mich. 48018.

The Yale Review, ed. J. D. McClatchy. P.O. Box 1902A, Yale Station, New Haven, Conn. 06520.

ZYZZYVA, ed. Howard Junker. 41 Sutter Street, Suite 1400, San Francisco, Calif. 94104.

ACKNOWLEDGMENTS

Grateful acknowledgment is made to the publications from which the poems in this volume were chosen. Unless specifically noted otherwise, copyright of the poems is held by the individual poets.

Jonathan Aaron: "Dance Mania" appeared in *The Paris Review*. Reprinted by permission of the poet.

Agha Shahid Ali: "I See Chile in My Rearview Mirror" from *A Nostalgist's Map of America* by Agha Shahid Ali (W. W. Norton & Co., Inc., 1991). Copyright © 1991 by Agha Shahid Ali. The poem appeared first in *Field*. Reprinted by permission of the poet.

John Ash: "The Ungrateful Citizens" from *The Burnt Pages* by John Ash (Random House, 1991). Copyright © 1991 by John Ash. Reprinted by permission. The poem appeared in *The Paris Review*.

John Ashbery: "Poem at the New Year" appeared in *The New Yorker*, February 11, 1991. Reprinted by permission; © 1991 John Ashbery.

Robin Behn: "Midwestern Villanelle" appeared in *The Iowa Review*. Reprinted by permission of the poet.

Charles Bernstein: "How I Painted Certain of My Pictures" appeared in *Hambone*. Reprinted by permission of the poet.

George Bilgere: "Healing" appeared in *The Iowa Review*. Reprinted by permission of the poet.

Elizabeth Bishop: "Poem" ("Dear, my compass . . .") originally in *The New Yorker*, September 30, 1991. Copyright © 1991 by Alice Helen Methfessel. Reprinted by permission of Farrar, Straus & Giroux, Inc. Lloyd Schwartz's comments, originally in *The New Yorker*, reprinted by permission.

Robert Bly: "The Crippled Godwit" appeared in *Ploughshares*. Reprinted by permission of the poet.

Lucie Brock-Broido: "Inevitably, She Declined" appeared in *Michigan Quarterly Review*. Reprinted by permission of the poet.

Joseph Brodsky: "Homage to Gerolamo Marcello" originally in *The New Yorker*, January 21, 1991. Reprinted by permission; © 1991 Joseph Brodsky.

Hayden Carruth: "Sex" from *The Sewanee Review*. Reprinted by permission of the poet.

Billy Collins: "Nostalgia" from *The Georgia Review* and, subsequently, *Questions about Angels* (Morrow, 1991). Reprinted by permission of the poet.

Other books in this series are available at your local bookstore or by mail. To order directly, return the coupon below to Macmillan Publishing Company, Special Sales Department, 866 Third Avenue, New York, NY 10022.

Line Sequence	ISBN	Title	Price	Quantity
1	0-02-044182-7	THE BEST AMERICAN POETRY 1989 (paper) edited by Donald Hall	$9.95	___
2	0-02-032785-4	THE BEST AMERICAN POETRY 1990 (paper) edited by Jorie Graham	$11.00	___
3	0-684-19311-6	THE BEST AMERICAN POETRY 1991 (cloth) edited by Mark Strand	$27.95	___
4	0-02-069844-5	THE BEST AMERICAN POETRY 1991 (paper) edited by Mark Strand	$12.95	___

Subtotal ___

Please add postage and handling costs—$1.50 for the first book and 50¢ for each additional book ___

Sales tax—if applicable ___

TOTAL ___

Lines Units

___ Enclosed is my check/money order payable to Macmillan Publishing Company.

Bill my ___ AMEX ___ MasterCard ___ Visa   Control No. [   ]   Ord. Type [SPCA]

Card # _____

Expiration date _____ Signature _____   For charge orders only:

Charge orders valid only with signature

Ship to: _____   Bill to: _____

_____   _____

_____ Zip Code   _____ Zip Code

For information regarding bulk purchases, please write to Special Sales Director at the above address. Publisher's prices and availability are subject to change without notice.

PSL/PSR 804